Growing up Modern

For Kai

This book is made possible, in part, by the New York State Council on the Arts with the support of Governor Andrew M. Cuomo and the New York State Legislature.

NEW YORK STATE OF OPPORTUNITY. | Council on the Arts

Elise Jaffe + Jeffrey Brown

MIT School of Architecture and Planning

Julia Jamrozik
Coryn Kempster

Growing up Modern

Childhoods in Iconic Homes

BIRKHÄUSER
BASEL

Graphic design, layout and typesetting
Miriam Bussmann

Copy editing
Jayne Kelley

Project management
Ria Stein

Production
Heike Strempel

Paper
Amber Graphic 120 g/m²

Cloth
Printa, Bamberger Kaliko

Printing
Eberl & Kœsel Fine Prints, Altusried

Library of Congress Control Number: 2020946438
Bibliographic information published by the German National Library
The German National Library lists this publication in the Deutsche Nationalbibliografie; detailed bibliographic data are available on the Internet at http://dnb.dnb.de.

ISBN 978-3-0356-1905-8
e-ISBN (PDF) 978-3-0356-2031-3

This book is also available in a German language edition with the title *Kinder der Moderne*, ISBN 978-3-0356-2167-9;
e-ISBN (PDF) 978-3-0356-2168-6.

P.O. Box 44, 4009 Basel, Switzerland
Part of Walter de Gruyter GmbH, Berlin/Boston
9 8 7 6 5 4 3 2 1

www.birkhauser.com

Contents

"Memories of the outside world will never have
the same tonality as those of home and, by recalling
these memories, we add to our store of dreams;
we are never real historians, but always near poets,
and our emotion is perhaps nothing but an
expression of a poetry that was lost."

Gaston Bachelard

Architecture and Personal Narrative

Introduction

What was it like to grow up in an early Modernist villa or housing estate?

Did living in such settings change children's attitudes? Did these radical environments shape the way they looked at domestic space later in life? Were children in Modernist homes self-conscious about their avant-garde surroundings, or proud of them?

To answer these questions, this book looks directly to a group of individuals who were the first inhabitants of radical Modernist domestic spaces as children. We documented their memories in an effort to understand the impact, or lack thereof, that these buildings had on our interlocutors at the time, as well as the influence, if any, they continue to have on their adult selves. Moreover, we wanted to understand the buildings themselves from the perspectives of their users—not as sterile monuments or architectural visions, but as places that harbored life, and in many ways continue to do so. The stories presented here offer an aggregation of individual memories that differ in circumstances, intensity, and details, and which have all inevitably faded with the passage of time. They nevertheless paint a uniquely intimate portrait of Modernism. Despite the volume of research and publications devoted to the buildings this book covers and the architects who designed them, approaching these masterworks through oral history helped us uncover aspects of the projects that have not yet been recorded.

To speak with the children who first inhabited these buildings, and not the adults, was crucial for us. Beyond the practical impossibility of speaking to residents who have long since passed away, the adults chose either to commission or to live in the avant-garde settings and might therefore be partisan to them.[2] Instead, we sought the perspectives of their children, who we imagined were more open-minded and less inhibited. We were fortunate to interview Rolf Fassbaender, Ernst Tugendhat, Helga Zumpfe, and Gisèle Moreau, original inhabitants, respectively, of a row house by J. J. P. Oud in the Weissenhof Estate, in Stuttgart, Germany (1927); the Tugendhat House, by Ludwig Mies van der Rohe, in Brno, Czech Republic (1930); the Schminke House, by Hans Scharoun, in Löbau, Germany (1933); and Le Corbusier's Unité d'Habitation apartments in Marseille, France (1952). As part of the project, we also visited our interlocutors' childhood dwellings and documented them through photographs that reflect their recollections.

Visiting places like the Weissenhof Estate, completed more than ninety years ago, it is hard to imagine just how radical buildings by early Modernist architects must have first appeared. Photographs from the time depicting the latest automobile designs and clothing fashions provide a hint, as does the passionate criticism that Modernist architecture received in its day. These structures were truly revolutionary, not only in their formal or aesthetic expression, but more fundamentally in the new way of living that they represented and promoted. Modernist buildings were also political, used to channel social visions and convey an idea of liberation from the conventions of the past.

Henry-Russell Hitchcock and Philip Johnson, the curators of *Modern Architecture: International Exhibition*, a seminal exhibition held at the Museum of Modern Art in New York in 1932, defined three aesthetic qualities of the new architecture: "There is, first, a new conception of architecture as volume rather than as mass. Secondly, regularity rather than axial symmetry serves as the chief means of ordering design. ... A third proscrib[es] arbitrarily applied decoration."[3] Yet it was Modernism's progressive aspirations that defined the movement as not just an architectural style but also a way of operating in the world. There was an implied duty to express the zeitgeist, the "spirit of an age," as Nikolaus Pevsner wrote,[4] advancing a radical, even moral agenda to reshape society through architecture.[5] As Sarah Williams Goldhagen points out, "Modernism in architecture was and is an ongoing conversation, a discussion about how, in living with the cultural, political, social, and economic conditions of modernity, a newly conceptualized built environment might enhance self-awareness, might improve social life, might contribute to a more humanized present, and might help people to envision their future in a better world."[6] Le Corbusier and other Modernists believed that architecture could have a transformative effect on society and on the individual. The dwelling or the "machine for living" was a vehicle for architectural explorations as well as social impact. "The problem of the house is a problem of the epoch. The equilibrium of society today depends on it," Le Corbusier wrote in his 1923 manifesto *Towards a New Architecture*. "Architecture has for its first duty, in this period of renewal, that of bringing about a revision of values, a revision of the constituent elements of the house."[7]

Much has been written about the Modernist architects' claims of bringing about social change and the fulfillment (or failure) of these lofty ambitions. Our aim is neither to prove nor disprove the success of these buildings in this context; our project is not a quantitative study of the influence of architecture on its inhabitants,[8] nor an assessment of Modernism's wider social effects. Rather, it is an attempt to record the personal, unique, and fleeting memories of people whose childhood surroundings, through luck or the directed efforts of their parents, were unconventional. While it may be difficult to divorce the impact of architecture from its socioeconomic or cultural contexts or the ideals of those who inhabited it, it is nevertheless worthwhile to examine these buildings from a point of view, that of the user, that has not been common in architectural history.[9]

Publishing these stories allows both architects and those interested in architecture to view these iconic buildings from another perspective, prompting readers to imagine design through the eyes of children and more generally through the eyes of the user. The goal of the research behind *Growing up Modern* has been to challenge ourselves, and our audience, to better understand the visionary and political agency of architecture, not by denying the fact that architectural spaces are functional—that their histories are multifaceted and not controlled by the architect—but precisely by embracing this reality.

"Oral history interviews might have the capacity to puncture through architecture's professional mask and bring to the fore unauthorized, polyphonic, human, and social narratives," Naomi Stead and Janina Gosseye suggest.[10] By giving voice to not only the architect but also others involved in the processes of producing and using architecture, Stead and Gosseye argue for the value of oral history as a methodology in the writing of deeper and broader architectural history. While many institutions have accumulated interviews with significant architects and landscape architects,[11] the perspective of the user has typically remained uninvestigated.[12]

Using oral history methods,[13] our research consisted of a close reading of dialogues and material artifacts. It acknowledges the personal and subjective impacts of the interaction between narrator and interviewer; our individual and collective biases are more or less willingly tangled into the narratives, just as they are present in the framing of each photograph. The circumstances of the informal conversations, the language barriers or errors of translation, the ambiguity of unspoken gestures and implied connotations—all are embedded in the stories produced as part of this volume. The material is marked by the imperfections of this method, yet we believe it is also greatly enriched by them, ultimately allowing for a fresh and intimate look at these iconic structures. In the book *Speaking of Buildings*, Gosseye, Stead, and Deborah van der Plaat argue that "by documenting the experience of and interactions with buildings over time, oral history can give a dynamic fourth dimension to (what are generally thought of as) static three-dimensional structures."[14]

In her book *House as a Mirror of Self*, Clare Cooper Marcus emphasizes the ties we have to the spaces we grow up in: "As we change and grow throughout our lives, our psychological development is punctuated not only by meaningful emotional relationships with people, but also by close affective ties with a number of significant physical environments, beginning in childhood."[15] Through an analysis based on the ideas of Carl Jung, Marcus elaborates on the complex forms of attachment and self-representation that develop from the domestic spaces we occupy, spaces of childhood in particular. Indeed, childhood, a "time of acute vulnerability and openness,"[16] is also a formative period in the development of one's relationship to the world and its structures, both physical and implied. Marcus speaks of memories and dreams as a "personal 'library'" and calls childhood memories "a kind of psychic anchor, reminding us of where we come from."[17]

The philosopher Gaston Bachelard goes further, arguing that "over and beyond our memories, the house we were born in is physically inscribed in us."[18] In his view, the elements of our first house imprint on our unconscious and physical memory, forming a personal definition of architecture generally.[19] The childhood home becomes a prototypical space, a foundational reference, as we encounter the world beyond the shelter of early domesticity. Even more than physical characteristics like dimensions, materials, or textures, however, it is the synthetic nature of the childhood home that gives it an almost mythical quality for Bachelard: "All I ought to say about my childhood home is just barely enough to place me, myself, in an oneiric situation, to set me on the threshold of a day-dream in which I shall find repose in the past."[20] Daydreams triggered by thoughts of a childhood home synthetize physical spaces with events that occurred in them, layering on the subsequent experiences and feelings of those dreaming. Bachelard thus claims that "the house is one of the greatest powers of integration for the thoughts, memories and dreams of mankind."[21]

"The voyage into the landscapes of childhood is not a return to objective features, but rather a journey as the adult self into the childhood self," Rachel

Sebba explains in presenting her research into spatial memories of childhood.[22] The recollections in *Growing up Modern* were necessarily colored by our interlocutors' subsequent experiences and the historical events surrounding them. A mixture of trauma and nostalgia related to the displacement of families during and after World War II, in particular, plays a large part in their stories, straining, tainting, or glorifying memories of their childhood environments.

Tonya Davidson links the memories of inhabitants and the physical structure of a house in a direct way: "The care and construction that produce houses as spaces of dwelling also produce houses as places that remember," the sociologist writes.[23] This connection is a critical one, as it relocates the recollections we have gathered from the realm of personal narrative into the more public realms of preservation and scholarship. Davidson uses Alison Landsberg's notion of "prosthetic memories" to describe the memories of others as means of gaining access to a time and place that one has not personally experienced.[24] The stories of these houses' past inhabitants can provide prosthetic memories of both individual experiences as well as the broader zeitgeist. The narratives thus look at the past from a collective and contemporary perspective, adding visceral understanding and empathy to our ideas of heritage.

Not every person we spoke with had strong or fond memories of their childhood home. Their feelings and attitudes ranged from embarrassment and apathy to admiration and nostalgia. For the individuals who still live in the houses or apartments of their childhood, memories have become intertwined with current preoccupations or have been inflected by the recognized significance of the architecture. Nevertheless, the presence of the houses in our interlocutors' personal archives, and even in some of their dreams, speaks to the bond between dwelling and occupant. This link, as Davidson argues, is not one-sided. The value of buildings as historical and architectural landmarks is only augmented by the narratives of their occupation, their changing use, and their inhabitants' associated perceptions over time. The individuals we spoke with are linked to the buildings through personal experiences, but the buildings are equally saturated with the evolving complexities of occupation.

The subjective and partial memories of past inhabitants are rich in anecdotal detail and speak to the messy life of architecture beyond its inception and construction. Although the passage of time can blur or exaggerate these memories, it is important to keep in mind that the memories of the architects who designed the buildings are equally fallible.[25] The fragmentary nature of human recollection means that the elements and spaces that were most impactful—or those remembered as most impactful—come to the fore in the stories we gathered. "Memories are motionless, and the more securely they are fixed in space, the sounder they are," Bachelard writes.[26] The interplay between a memory and an architectural detail, such as Rolf Fassbaender's bedroom balcony or the colored portholes in the doors of Helga Zumpfe's home, speaks most clearly to the value of this form of personal architectural narrative. In all the conversations, the act of recollecting everyday memories exposed new ways of understanding the spaces of these seminal houses. In revisiting specific spatial configurations and their associated social dynamics, the narrators communicate both factual and emotive characteristics of these well-known domestic spaces. Such complexity and richness, inaccessible through other historical approaches or site visits, proves the value of oral history in understanding architecture.

Growing up Modern is based on a series of conversations we had in 2015. That summer, we traveled with our nine-month-old son on a route linking the Modernist houses and the current dwellings of our interlocutors.[27] While initially we undertook our preliminary research independently by looking through historical records (often obituaries), many of the interviews were arranged with the help of museums or foundations, such as the Weissenhofmuseum, the Fondation Le Corbusier, and the Stiftung Haus Schminke. We conducted the conversations with Ernst Tugendhat and Helga Zumpfe in their current homes; Rolf Fassbaender spoke to us in a unit identical to his childhood home; for Gisèle Moreau, her childhood and current homes are one and the same. Whether during the conversations or on a separate visit, it was interesting to experience the varying statuses of these Modernist homes today. While the Tugendhat House and the Schminke House have been turned into museums, most remaining buildings of the Weissenhof Estate and the apartments of the Unité d'Habitation are still in use as housing. We were also fortunate to have the opportunity to stay overnight in the hotel of the Unité d'Habitation and in the Schminke House, which can be rented after museum hours.

In addition to summarizing each meeting and the stories brought out through our conversations, each chapter in this book includes basic information about the dwelling and its architectural significance as well as the architect's drawings of the house. Complementing the recollections are annotated drawings locating places and events mentioned during the interviews as well as photographic documentation of the dwelling, created with a specific focus on illustrating the aspects of the homes that were significant in the inhabitant's memories. The chapters are arranged chronologically based on the year of the building's completion.

Weissenhof Estate Row House
J. J. P. Oud—Stuttgart, Germany, 1927
Conversation with Rolf Fassbaender

This chapter conveys the experiences of Rolf Fassbaender, who lived with his mother at Pankokweg 3 from the opening of the Weissenhof Estate, in 1927, until 1939. Mr. Fassbaender's memories of the row house involve both the immediate exterior of the house, with its sunny garden and service court, and the larger neighborhood. The interiors of the unit, such as the social space of the living room and especially the balcony off Mr. Fassbaender's bedroom (where he could sleep under the stars), also figure prominently in his narrative.

Tugendhat House
Ludwig Mies van der Rohe—Brno, Czech Republic, 1930
Conversation with Ernst Tugendhat

The second chapter focuses on the memories that Ernst Tugendhat, a retired professor of philosophy, shared during our conversation. Of the surviving Tugendhat children, he is the only one old enough to have inhabited the famous house in Brno, which the family was forced to leave when he was only eight years old. Even the most idiosyncratic of the rooms in the villa did not leave a lasting impression on our interlocutor, whose memories instead revolve around the house's exterior spaces. He was aware, however, of the extravagant and opulent qualities of the house and his own feelings about it.

Schminke House
Hans Scharoun—Löbau, Germany, 1933
Conversation with Helga Zumpfe

Helga Zumpfe, the youngest of the Schminke children, spent her childhood in the house in Löbau. This chapter presents her descriptions of the spaces and details of the house and the effects they had on her, both growing up and as an adult. She still dreams of the house and credits the experiences she had there for informing many personal and professional aspects of her later life. Her recollections further highlight the strong and lasting friendship that developed between the architect and the family.

Unité d'Habitation
Le Corbusier—Marseille, France, 1952
Conversation with Gisèle Moreau

This chapter is based on our interview with Gisèle Moreau, who moved into Le Corbusier's Unité d'Habitation in Marseille when it opened and has resided there for the majority of her life. She has lived in several apartments in the building but now occupies the apartment in which she grew up, having inherited it from her parents. She is passionately invested in telling the story of the building that has become a significant aspect of her, and her family's, identity.

In choosing the architecture represented in this book, we considered the most iconic examples of Modernism—buildings that would be familiar to most architects and architecture enthusiasts. We consciously included different types of dwelling, such as villas, a row house, and an apartment, in order to represent a myriad of scenarios and experiences, typologies and socioeconomic circumstances. Sadly, several individuals with whom we wanted to speak for the study are no longer alive;[28] there were also important houses that had no children among their first occupants. These facts necessarily conditioned the study and the stories that we were able to collect. It was also important for the consistency of the study to photograph the childhood homes of those we spoke to in a manner that was informed by their perspectives. For that reason, we have not included the conversations we conducted with Mrs. Goron, who grew up in a house designed by Le Corbusier in the Cité Frugès, in Pessac, or with Hans Reif, who grew up in a Walter Gropius–designed house in the Weissenhof Estate that was destroyed during World War II. While both fascinating in their own ways, these components of the study remained incomplete because we could not access the dwellings themselves.

By focusing on lived experiences of the user as opposed to the formal, tectonic, theoretical, or myriad other concerns that typically form the backbone of architectural history (of Modernism as much as that of other periods), *Growing up Modern* calls into question which histories of exemplary structures are being preserved. It posits that the intimate recollections of those who have occupied the buildings over the course of their existence, especially the stories of their first inhabitants, are as valid and worthy of preservation as the reflections of their creators, the critiques of contemporaries and historians, and the material constructions themselves. Through its sustained attention to childhood experiences of Modernist domesticity, *Growing up Modern* contributes to an expanded and evolving architectural and social history.

Notes

1 Gaston Bachelard, *The Poetics of Space* (New York: Orion Press, 1964), 6. (Source for quotation on p. 6)

2 The perspectives of the parents are often already recorded, especially in the cases of commissioned single-family homes. See, for example, Grete Tugendhat and Fritz Tugendhat, "The Inhabitants of the Tugendhat House Give Their Opinion," letter to the editor, *Die Form* 6, no. 11, November 15, 1931, reprinted and translated in Daniela Hammer-Tugendhat, Ivo Hammer, and Wolf Tegethoff, *Tugendhat House: Ludwig Mies van der Rohe*, new ed. (Basel: Birkhäuser, 2015), 76–77. For the role and perspective of female clients in particular, see Alice T. Friedman, *Women and the Making of the Modern House: A Social and Architectural History* (New York: Harry N. Abrams, 1998).

3 Henry-Russell Hitchcock Jr. and Philip Johnson, *The International Style: Architecture since 1922* (New York: W. W. Norton, 1932), 20.

4 Nikolaus Pevsner, *An Outline of European Architecture*, 7th ed. (1943; repr., Harmondsworth, UK: Penguin, 1963), 17.

5 Ed Taverne, Cor Wagenaar, and Martien de Vletter, *J. J. P. Oud: Poetic Functionalist, 1890–1963; The Complete Works* (Rotterdam: NAi Publishers, 2001), 34.

6 Sarah Williams Goldhagen, "Something to Talk About: Modernism, Discourse, Style," *Journal of the Society of Architectural Historians* 64, no. 2 (June 2005): 163.

7 Le Corbusier, *Towards a New Architecture*, trans. Frederick Etchells (1931; repr., New York: Dover Publications, 1986), 6.

8 Either in the vein of quantitative post-occupancy evaluations or the more conceptual approach presented by AMO and Rem Koolhaas in their guest-edited *Domus* issue "Post-Occupancy" (2006).

9 "If a lot of architecture's meaning is made not on the drafting board but in the complex lifeworld of how it is inhabited, consumed, used, lived or neglected, that world is at once central and peculiarly under-explored." Kenny Cupers, *Use Matters: An Alternative History of Architecture* (London: Routledge, 2013), 1. See also Stephen Grabow and Kent F. Spreckelmeyer, *The Architecture of Use: Aesthetics and Function in Architectural Design* (New York: Routledge, 2015). In recent years, several significant books and exhibitions have focused on design for children, including Amy F. Ogata, *Designing the Creative Child: Playthings and Places in Midcentury America* (Minneapolis: University of Minnesota Press, 2013); Alexandra Lange, *The Design of Childhood: How the Material World Shapes Independent Kids* (New York: Bloomsbury Press, 2018); and the 2012 Museum of Modern Art exhibition *Century of the Child: Growing by Design, 1900–2000*, and its associated catalogue, Juliet Kinchin and Aidan O'Connor, *Century of the Child: Growing by Design, 1900–2000* (New York: Museum of Modern Art, 2012).

10 "Oral History, Part I: Methods and Mistakes," video recording of a seminar led by Gosseye and Stead at the Canadian Centre for Architecture, July 4, 2017,

27:57, https://www.cca.qc.ca/en/events/50476/oral-history-part-i-methods-and-mistakes.

11 Including the Archives of American Art, the British Library, the UCLA Library, and the Art Institute of Chicago, among others. See also John Peter, *The Oral History of Modern Architecture: Interviews with the Greatest Architects of the Twentieth Century* (New York: Harry N. Abrams, 1994).

12 Significant exceptions are Philippe Boudon, *Lived-In Architecture: Le Corbusier's Pessac Revisited*, trans. Gerald Onn (Cambridge, MA: MIT Press, 1972); Danielle Aubert, Lana Cavar, and Natasha Chandani, eds., *Thanks for the View, Mr. Mies: Lafayette Park, Detroit* (New York: Metropolis Books, 2012), which focuses primarily on contemporary occupants of Lafayette Park, but also brings forth historical information based on the stories of long-term residents; Esra Akcan, *Open Architecture: Migration, Citizenship and the Urban Renewal of Berlin-Kreuzberg by IBA 1984/87* (Basel: Birkhäuser, 2018); Hilde de Haan and Jolanda Keesom, *What Happened to My Buildings: Learning from 30 Years of Architecture with Marlies Rohmer* (Rotterdam: nai010, 2016); and essays in Janina Gosseye, Naomi Stead, and Deborah van der Plaat, eds., *Speaking of Buildings: Oral History in Architectural Research* (New York: Princeton Architectural Press, 2019).

13 We are not oral historians and have not been formally trained in the practice, though we have attended oral history workshops at Columbia University. We refer to significant texts on the practice of oral history in our efforts to not only record but also transcribe and represent the stories that our interlocutors narrated to us as part of this project. See Donald A. Ritchie, *Doing Oral History: A Practical Guide*, 2nd ed. (Oxford, UK: Oxford University Press, 2003); Robert Perks and Alistair Thomson, *The Oral History Reader*, 2nd ed. (London: Routledge, 2006); and Gosseye, Stead, and van der Plaat, *Speaking of Buildings*.

14 Gosseye, Stead, and van der Plaat, *Speaking of Buildings*, 26.

15 Clare Cooper Marcus, *House as a Mirror of Self: Exploring the Deeper Meaning of Home* (Berkeley, CA: Conari, 1995), 4.

16 Marcus, *House as a Mirror of Self*, 34.

17 Marcus, *House as a Mirror of Self*, 41, 20.

18 Bachelard, *Poetics of Space*, 14.

19 We take "first house" to mean not necessarily the house one is born in or occupied from birth, but more poignantly the house with which one associates one's most lasting early impressions.

20 Bachelard, *Poetics of Space*, 13.

21 Bachelard, *Poetics of Space*, 6.

22 Rachel Sebba, "The Landscapes of Childhood: The Reflection of Childhood's Environment in Adult Memories and in Children's Attitudes," *Environment and Behavior* 23, no. 4 (July 1991): 419.

23 Tonya Davidson, "The Role of Domestic Architecture in the Structuring of Memory," *Space and Culture* 12, no. 3 (August 2009): 334.

24 See Alison Landsberg, *Prosthetic Memory: The Transformation of American Remembrance in the Age of Mass Culture* (New York: Columbia University Press, 2004).

25 For an examination of issues related to the architect interview as a historical method, see Robert Procter, "The Architect's Intention: Interpreting Post-War Modernism through the Architect Interview," *Journal of Design History* 19, no. 4 (Winter 2006): 295–307.

26 Bachelard, *Poetics of Space*, 9.

27 We elaborate on this aspect of the project in the conclusion of this book. Our personal reflections on the trip and having our child be part of the research (and in some ways part of the conversations) are also documented in "Growing up Modern: A Family Story," *MAS Context* 32, "Character" (2019).

28 Our study was spurred by a visit to Le Corbusier's Villa Savoye, on the outskirts of Paris, in the fall of 2005. We were struck by the notes and letters of Eugénie Savoye, which describe in minute detail both the programmatic intentions and the built inadequacies of the house. We were particularly taken by her mention of her son Roger, whose pneumonia, she claimed, was caused by the cold and leaky conditions of the weekend home. This caused us to wonder what the child's memories of the place were and how he would recall the spaces of the iconic Modernist villa. Roger Savoye had passed long before he could be interviewed for this study, but correspondence with his son Jean-Marc revealed that Roger was actually 21 years old when Le Corbusier completed the house (email exchange with the authors, May 9, 2015). For the perspective of Jean-Marc Savoye on the famous house, see Jean-Philippe Delhomme and Jean-Marc Savoye, *The Sunny Days of Villa Savoye* (Basel: Birkhäuser, 2020).

Weissenhof Estate Row House

J.J.P. Oud
Stuttgart, Germany
1927

Jacobus Johannes Pieter (J.J.P.) Oud was the first of seventeen architects whom artistic director Ludwig Mies van der Rohe invited to take part in the Weissenhof Estate, or Weissenhofsiedlung, an experimental housing exhibition sited on a hill overlooking Stuttgart that opened in 1927 (fig. 1). Organized by the Deutscher Werkbund and sponsored by the city of Stuttgart, the Weissenhof Estate was a demonstration project that lauded the development and implementation of new ideas of functionality, new construction techniques, and new ways of living. The historical importance of this event cannot be overestimated; it not only consolidated many facets of Modernism in architecture, but also proved to be a pivotal social moment within and beyond Germany, eliciting both praise and criticism of the ideals behind the exhibition's dominant aesthetic—what became known as the International Style.[1]

At the time, Oud was already a respected Modernist architect and had completed numerous social housing and other projects in his native Holland.[2] His contribution to the Weissenhof Estate was a set of five identical row houses, each with a front garden and a service courtyard toward the street, which were intended for the "sensible, solid, middle class."[3]

The architect took great care in the planning of the houses and focused especially on everyday use. His ideas were based on materials provided by the exhibition curators: efficient home plans drawn up by Stuttgart housewives and guidelines for the kitchen and kitchen fittings by Erna Meyer, the author of the 1925 book *Der*

▲ An aerial view of the Weissenhofsiedlung during the exhibition, 1927. [1]
▼ Row houses photographed from the south (garden) side. [2]

neue Haushalt (The New Household).[4] As Ed Taverne, Cor Wagenaar, and Martien de Vletter explain, "Oud's plans, by contrast [to those of Le Corbusier], were warmly received by Erna Meyer and they formed the basis of an intensive and extremely professional exchange of ideas between the architect and the home economist. As a result, Oud was able to refine his dwelling ... until it was a veritable 'Ford home', a model of domestic efficiency."[5] To remain in line with Mies's overall design stipulations, Oud also incorporated the emblematic Modernist flat roof and white (or off-white) facade (figs. 2, 3).[6]

Oud's participation in the exhibition raised the status of the event but also helped earn him a prominent place in the history of Modernism in architecture. The architect had a "place of honour"[7] in the 1932 Museum of Modern Art exhibition *Modern Architecture: International Exhibition*: "The four leaders of modern architecture are Le Corbusier, Oud, Gropius and Mies van der Rohe," the exhibition's curators, Henry-Russell Hitchcock and Philip Johnson, proclaimed.[8]

▼ Row houses photographed from the north (Pankokweg) side. [3]

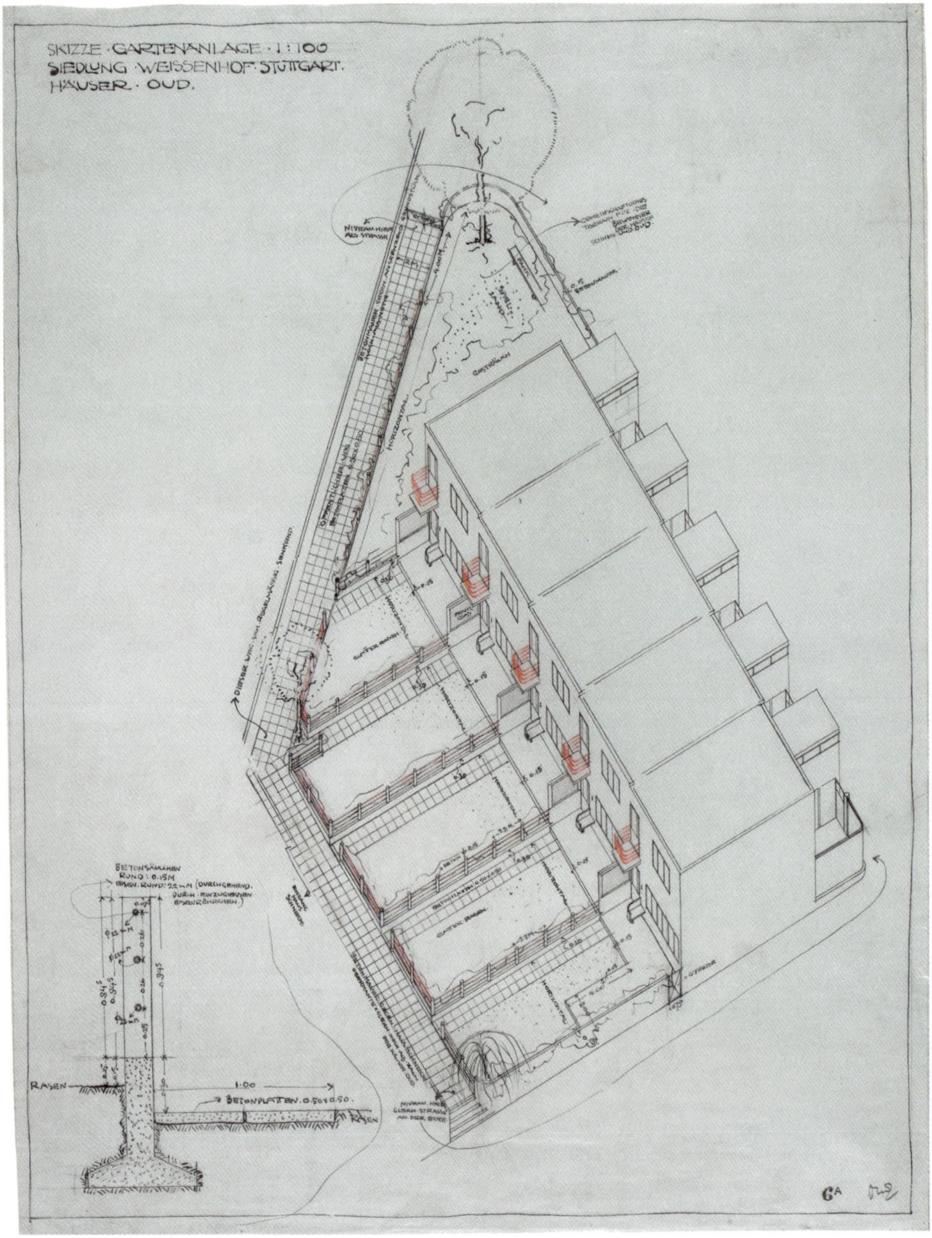

▲ An axonometric drawing of the row houses by J. J. P. Oud. **[4]**

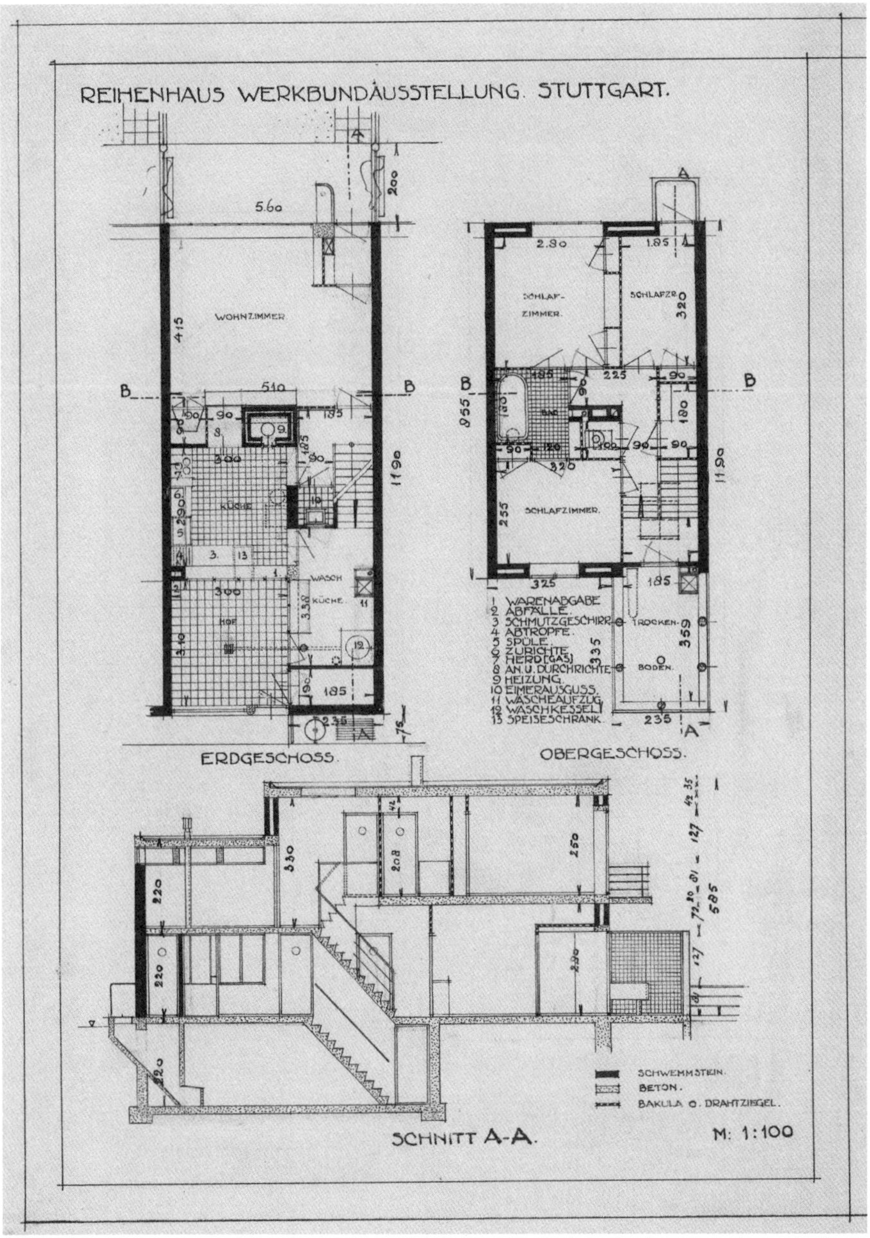

▲ Ground- and upper-level plans and section by J. J. P. Oud. [5]

Conversation with Rolf Fassbaender

Rolf Fassbaender lived at Pankokweg 3, one of the row houses designed by Oud in the Weissenhof Estate, from 1927 to 1939. "I have very, very good memories of my childhood here," he said of the house, which he affectionately referred to as "number 3" and described as "a very good, small, well-equipped apartment." The Weissenhofmuseum's director Anja Krämer arranged for us to speak with Mr. Fassbaender in Pankokweg 7, a row house identical to his childhood home. The row houses are still used as public housing; the unit where we met was awaiting renovations between tenants. Mr. Fassbaender answered our questions and gave us a tour of the row house and the Weissenhofsiedlung at large (figs. 29, 30). He also showed us family albums from his childhood and from a recent visit to the estate with his grandchildren (figs. 7, 20).

The construction of the row houses was completed in 1927; Mr. Fassbaender was two years old when his family moved into the dwelling. They had relocated from Aachen, where Rolf was born, when his father, who was a singer, received a contract with the theater in Stuttgart. A partnership between the city and the theater allowed the family to take residence in the Weissenhof Estate as the first inhabitants of the exhibition row houses.

◄ Rolf Fassbaender photographed in Pankokweg 7, a row house identical to his childhood home at the Weissenhofsiedlung, 2015. **[6]**
▼ A page from Mr. Fassbaender's childhood photo album showing him and his mother (center); the south facade and garden of "number 3," his childhood home (left); and him sledding on the small hill in front of the neighboring Ludwig Mies van der Rohe building (right). **[7]**

▲ Children from the Weissenhof Estate, including Rolf (top row, center). **[8]**

When his parents divorced a few years later, Rolf and his mother stayed in the house. At various times they were joined by two rabbits and the occasional architecture-student lodger. Though an only child, Rolf belonged to a large group of children in the neighborhood and developed strong bonds of friendship with many. "There was a family [who lived nearby] with eight children, and I was the ninth," he said. Photographs from the time show him with groups of children small and large, in his words "good friends, the best friends" (figs. 8–10).

The estate's buildings ranged from single-family villas to modest apartments. As a result, the neighborhood's inhabitants represented a mix of economic backgrounds, including intellectuals and musicians, such as Rolf's father and the cellist Hermann Busch, but also a policeman and other workers, as well as doctors and other wealthier professionals.[9] "A lot of Jewish people lived here, too," Mr. Fassbaender noted.

Though now surrounded by residential areas, at the time the Weissenhof Estate was on the outskirts of Stuttgart. The Weissenhof itself, which gave the area and later the housing estate its name, was a local farm, where Rolf would walk to get milk.[10]

▲ From left: Rolf (right) with a friend in front of the Mies van der Rohe apartment block, where they would play in the stairwells, and with a group of children (Rolf fourth from left) on the Pankokweg sidewalk by the Mies building. [9, 10]

▼ A view down Pankokweg showing the Oud row houses on the right and the Mies van der Rohe apartment block on the left, 1927. Hans Reif, another of the interlocutors for this study, lived in the Walter Gropius-designed House 17, seen in the center, from 1928 to 1932. The house was destroyed in World War II. [11]

▲ From left: Rolf with his pellet gun, which he used to shoot out the light of the lamppost on Pankokweg (see fig. 11); climbing the tree in the garden of his childhood row house; and with his rabbits, leaning against the row house's south facade. **[12–14]**

The children used the area's hilly pastures as football pitches. A public swimming pool and other sports facilities were also within walking distance.

The outdoor spaces of the row house and neighborhood are central to Mr. Fassbaender's memories, as they were the places where he spent most of his time playing. Standing on the street in front of his childhood home, looking out toward the estate's network of streets and paths, he exclaimed, "This was our playground!" With only three cars in the neighborhood at the time, the streets were still the domain of children (figs. 9–11, 35).

A concrete retaining wall at the northwest tip of the row houses was the spot where children would count while playing hide-and-seek (fig. 38). Preferred hiding places included the interconnected stairwells of the adjacent Mies van der Rohe–designed apartment block—one could enter the building, run through the basement level, and exit through another door. ("It was a lot of fun!" Mr. Fassbaender recalled.) Mr. Fassbaender also pointed to sites of boyhood mischief, such as the streetlight that shattered when he discovered, after several attempts, that his pellet gun was more powerful than he thought (figs. 11, 12, 37). Likewise, the stairwells in the Mies building, with their hard surfaces and vertical volumes, were a favorite location for setting off firecrackers; the spaces greatly amplified the sounds of the small explosions (fig. 36).

The south-facing front garden of "number 3" boasted the only tree among the row houses—a significant amenity, as "it was important to go up" (fig. 13). Mr. Fassbaender remembers sitting often on the concrete seat, a built-in appendage to the south facade of the house. "In summertime we had a table and a concrete bench, and life was lived outside," he recalled, recounting the time a bird swooped in and ate the butter off his sandwich (figs. 21, 24, 47, 48). The sunny garden, with its low perimeter wall, was also where he brought the rabbits (facetiously named Hitler and Hindenburg) on warm days from their regular home in the back, street-side enclosed service courtyard (figs. 14, 41).

Most architectural histories of the row houses focus on Oud's collaboration with the home economist Erna Meyer in the design of a modern kitchen (figs. 15–17, 42). Oud "made Erna Meyer's ideas about the location and layout of the kitchen and about rational household work the basis for his housing design," Taverne, Wagenaar, and de Vletter write.[11] For Mr. Fassbaender, however, the living room was the

▼ Views of the optimized kitchen of the row house, showing Rolf (center) and the pass-through from the kitchen to the dining and living space, which Mr. Fassbaender called the "umbilical cord" (far right). **[15–17]**

▲ From left: The round table in the living room of the Fassbaender row house, where the neighbors gathered in the evenings, and the radio and gramophone that stood in the living room by the entry vestibule, circa 1936. The photographer is presumed to be Mrs. Wittig, a friend of Rolf's mother's who worked in a photo studio in Stuttgart at the time. **[18, 19]**

most significant interior space: "The living room was the center of life." He described the passthrough between the kitchen and the living room, opened by sliding a panel, as "die Nabelschnur zur Küche"—an umbilical cord that tethered the spaces to one another, allowing the passage of objects and creating a strategic visual connection (fig. 17).

The living room faced the garden and held the gramophone, which Rolf used to project Plasticine cannonballs made from modeling materials gleaned from the student lodgers (fig. 19). More importantly, the room was a key social space for both adults and children in the neighborhood. Mr. Fassbaender's mother came from a large family in the Rhineland and was, he described, "the heart of the Pankokweg." She hosted the "Tischrunde Fassbaender," a regular gathering of neighbors around the room's circular table. "In the evening a lot of neighbors came. ... One brought his cheese and the other his meat; it was great!" he elaborated (figs. 18, 50).

▼ A page from Mr. Fassbaender's childhood photo album, with images of him sitting in the dining room of the row house with his mother (top row, second and third from left) and outside on the terrace with his parents (bottom row, first, second, and third from left). [20]

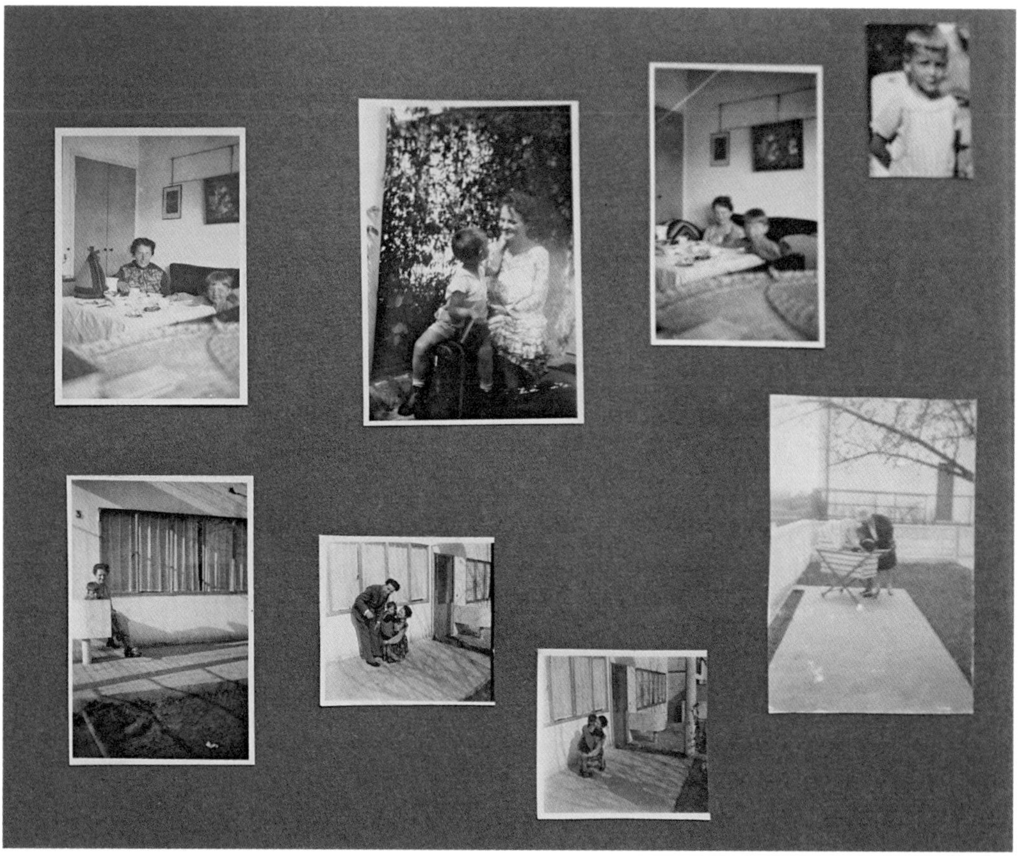

There was clearly a sense of community among neighbors in the estate but particularly between families in the row houses, including the children. Mr. Fassbaender recalled, for example, that he was familiar with the contents of the identical built-in sideboards of all the row houses, attesting to the access granted him to the living spaces of his neighbors. That intimacy was enhanced, and effectively imposed, by the poor acoustic isolation of the units. "The five [families] who lived in the row houses had to be on the same wavelength. The insulation against sound was not good. You could hear in number 3, 'Oh, [that's] the toilet in number 7,' ... 'Oh, number 9.' You could hear all big noises through all the units!" he remembered, laughing.

Walking through the row house as part of the interview, Mr. Fassbaender recollected with precise detail the many built-in cupboards and utility spaces, including the bookcase in the living room (which his family modified); the utility closet in the entrance, containing a tap for a garden hose; the walk-in linen cupboard at the top of the stairs, with attached shoe storage; and the set of bookcases flanking a make-

▼ Rolf kneeling on the concrete bench on the south facade of the row house (left) and balancing on neighbors' fences (center and right). **[21–23]**

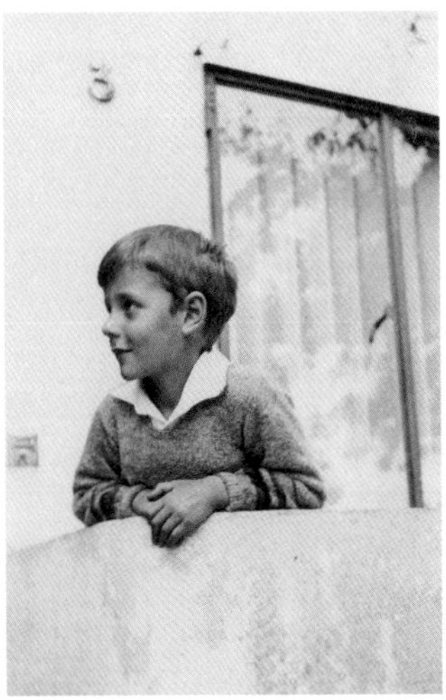

▲ A row house garden entrance with built-in concrete bench. The entrance canopy formed the base of a balcony off an upstairs bedroom (in Pankokweg 3, Rolf's room). **[24]**

up table in his mother's bedroom (figs. 30, 51). He remembered aspects of the dwelling that were altered over time, as well as idiosyncratic moments, such as the point on the upper level where three doors meet (from the hallway to the bathroom, the bathroom to what was his mother's bedroom, and the bedroom back to the hallway). He also recalled the location of the coal chute to the basement and the heating vents in each room, including one in the bathroom that he was especially happy to use to warm up after a bath (fig. 52).

The row houses also provide a dedicated laundry-drying room on a half-level between the living and sleeping spaces; Mr. Fassbaender speculated that Oud incorporated this feature because the Dutch architect was accustomed to a lot of rain. The continuous band of clerestory windows in this room not only allows ample cross ventilation, but also let Rolf sneakily call out to his friends playing on the street below before ducking out of view again (figs. 53, 54). A tennis ball once got stuck on the flat roof of the laundry drying room of "number 3," blocking the drain, and Mr. Fassbaender remembers flooding after a heavy rain, with water spilling down the stairs and even lifting a cupboard off the floor.

Most notably, Mr. Fassbaender passionately recalled the balcony of his room and the distinct spatial extension it enabled. As a projection not from the master bedroom but from the adjacent bedroom, the smallest in the house, the cantilevering concrete slab was likely conceived by the architect primarily from the exterior: as a canopy for the main entrance below, a demonstration of the capacities of reinforced concrete construction, or an element to enliven the south facade (fig. 24).[12] For the child, however, the projection transformed the experience of his bedroom entirely; as a boy, Mr. Fassbaender would drag the head of his mattress out onto the balcony on warm nights to "sleep under the sky, under the stars." This wonderful memory, enabled however unwittingly by the domestic architecture, is emblematic

▼ The nearby Brenzkirche, designed by Alfred Daiber, as completed in 1933 (left) and remodeled in 1939 (right). **[25, 26]**

▲ Rolf (left in both photos) with friends on the steps adjacent to one of Le Corbusier's houses. [27, 28]

of the generous functionality of the design (figs. 55–59). The arguable decadence of the row house balcony is matched by its imaginative use and lasting impression. While the avant-garde architectural setting seemed normal to Mr. Fassbaender as a boy and there was nothing about the house that he wished he could have changed, he was also aware that the architecture of the estate was unusual. Even after the exhibition was over, "a lot of people came to have a look," often peering into the private domestic spaces. Such visits became so frequent that the city eventually gated off the pedestrian path that runs past the gardens of the row houses, discouraging outsider access (fig. 44).

As the estate's buildings lacked what Mr. Fassbaender mockingly called the high-pitched "Nazi roof," less than a decade after construction, the National Socialist government deemed the Weissenhofsiedlung unrepresentative of its ideals of German identity. In 1933, a competing neighborhood with a supposedly truer "German style," Am Kochenhof, was built just to the west. Similarly in 1939, a neighboring Modernist church, Brenzkirche, was remodeled with a sloped roof and the

facade was modified to erase the distinctive curved corner and diagonal window of the stairway inside (figs. 25, 26). Speaking of Modernism in that time, Mr. Fassbaender said, "I could see that this style was not welcome."

Plans were drawn up to raze the entire Weissenhof Estate to establish a military command center,[13] and the Fassbaender family, like all inhabitants, was made to leave in 1939.[14] Rolf and his mother relocated to Sillenbuch, an area southeast of Stuttgart, and though the family purchased a plot of land, with the war underway in addition to financial constraints, they were not able to build a house on it. The area, which was surrounded by fields and woods, offered new opportunities to the boy. Mr. Fassbaender contends that many of the bonds and relationships formed in his time living in the Weissenhof Estate endured the move.

When asked about the impact of living in a Modernist row house and an ambitious experimental neighborhood, Mr. Fassbaender reflected, "There is an affinity, a connection between architecture and people living in it. ... [There's a] phrase not from architecture but you can translate into architecture: 'The outside of the horse forms the inside of the rider.'"

The house Mr. Fassbaender built for himself later in life, which he and his wife share with their son, daughter-in-law, and grandchildren, has a flat roof, but this decision was not a result of Weissenhof nostalgia—rather, the town's building regulations prohibit pitched roofs. While the house is unlike his childhood dwelling in other respects, there are nevertheless sensibilities that Mr. Fassbaender feels have carried through: "I think the memories from my living here in this region have been important for my ideas for my own house."

"I have always had good contact with architects and architecture, and I have had no difficulties to understand architecture and ... the idea to make a house in this way or in that way," Mr. Fassbaender explained. "For me, it's normal. But the roots of this are in my childhood living here. It gave a push for my whole life."

◀ Stills from Rolf Fassbaender's conversation with the authors, 2015. **[29]**

▶▶ Mr. Fassbaender visiting a row house with the same layout as his childhood home. **[30]**

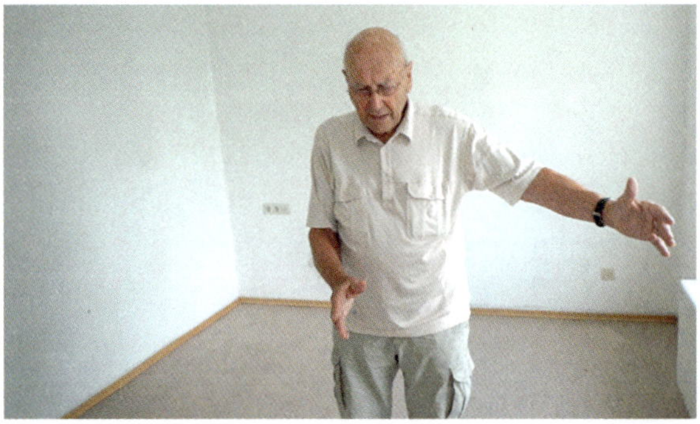

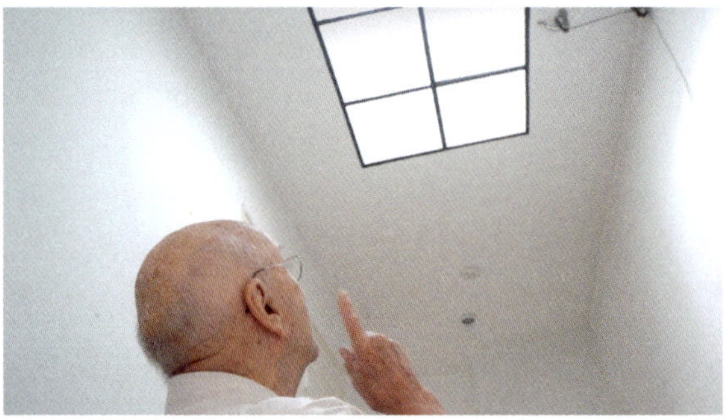

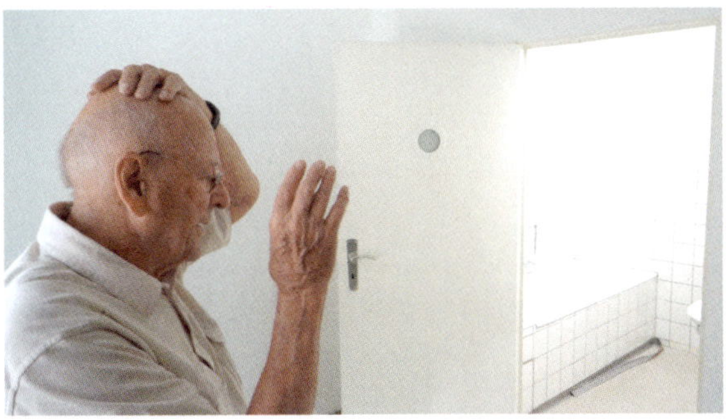

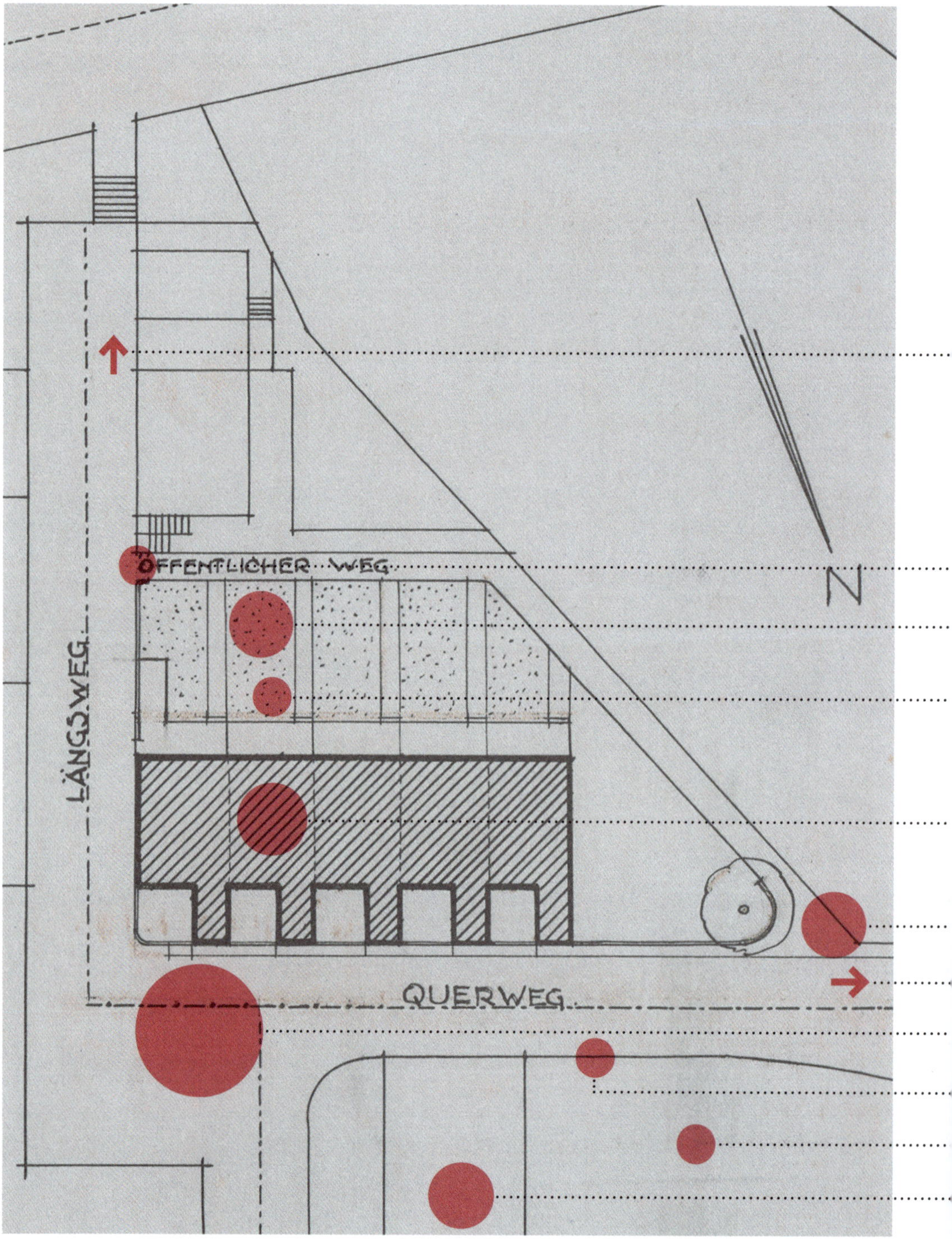
ÖFFENTLICHER WEG
LÄNGSWEG
QUERWEG
N

◀ A site plan with annotations referencing Mr. Fassbaender's memories. [31]

Path to the Weissenhof farm, where Rolf would get milk

Gates added after the exhibition to protect the inhabitants from onlookers

Garden "on the sunny side," where Rolf played with his friends and the rabbits (figs. 14, 44–46)

Tree that allowed the children to "go up" (fig. 13)

Number 3, Rolf Fassbaender's house

Small retaining wall, the counting place for hide-and-seek games (fig. 38)

Way to swimming pool

Pankokweg, labeled "Querweg" (Cross street) on Oud's site plan, the street that the children claimed as their playground (figs. 35, 39)

Streetlight that Rolf shot out with his pellet gun on Pankokweg (figs. 11, 12, 37)

Small hill for sledding (figs. 7, 36)

Mies van der Rohe building, with stairwells that were good places for hiding (going up and across on the roof or basement level and out another door) and setting off firecrackers (figs. 9, 10, 36)

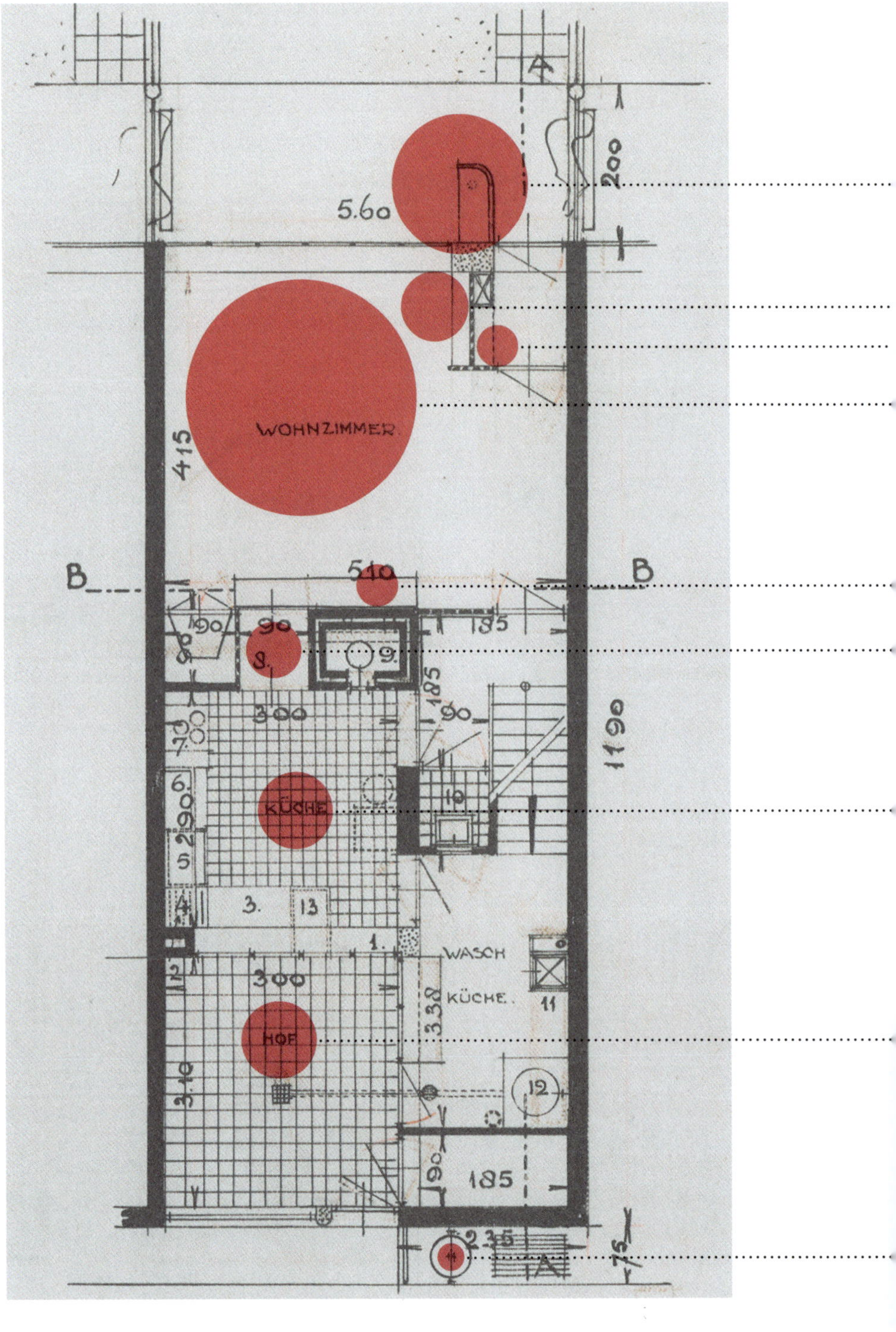

WOHNZIMMER
KÜCHE
WASCH
KÜCHE.
HOF
5.60
200
415
510
B
B
A
A
1190
300
300
185
185
3.38
3.10
2.35
75

◄ A ground-floor plan with annotations referencing Mr. Fassbaender's memories. **[32]**

Built-in concrete bench, where a bird ate the butter off of Rolf's bread (figs. 21, 24, 47, 48)

Location of the gramophone, which Rolf used to launch Plasticine cannonballs (figs. 19, 50)

Built-in utility closet with water tap for the garden (fig. 49)

Round table where neighbors would sit in the evenings for the "Tischrunde Fassbaender" (figs. 18, 50)

Built-in sideboard, identical in all the row houses, the contents of each of which Rolf knew well

Passthrough, which Mr. Fassbaender called "the umbilical cord" to the kitchen (figs. 17)

Kitchen, which receives the most attention from historians for its collaboration between Oud and Meyer but plays little role in Mr. Fassbaender's memories of the house (figs. 15–17, 42)

Street-side courtyard where Rolf's rabbits, facetiously named Hitler and Hindenburg, lived; they were brought to the garden on sunny days (figs. 14, 41–43)

Coal chute to the basement (fig. 35)

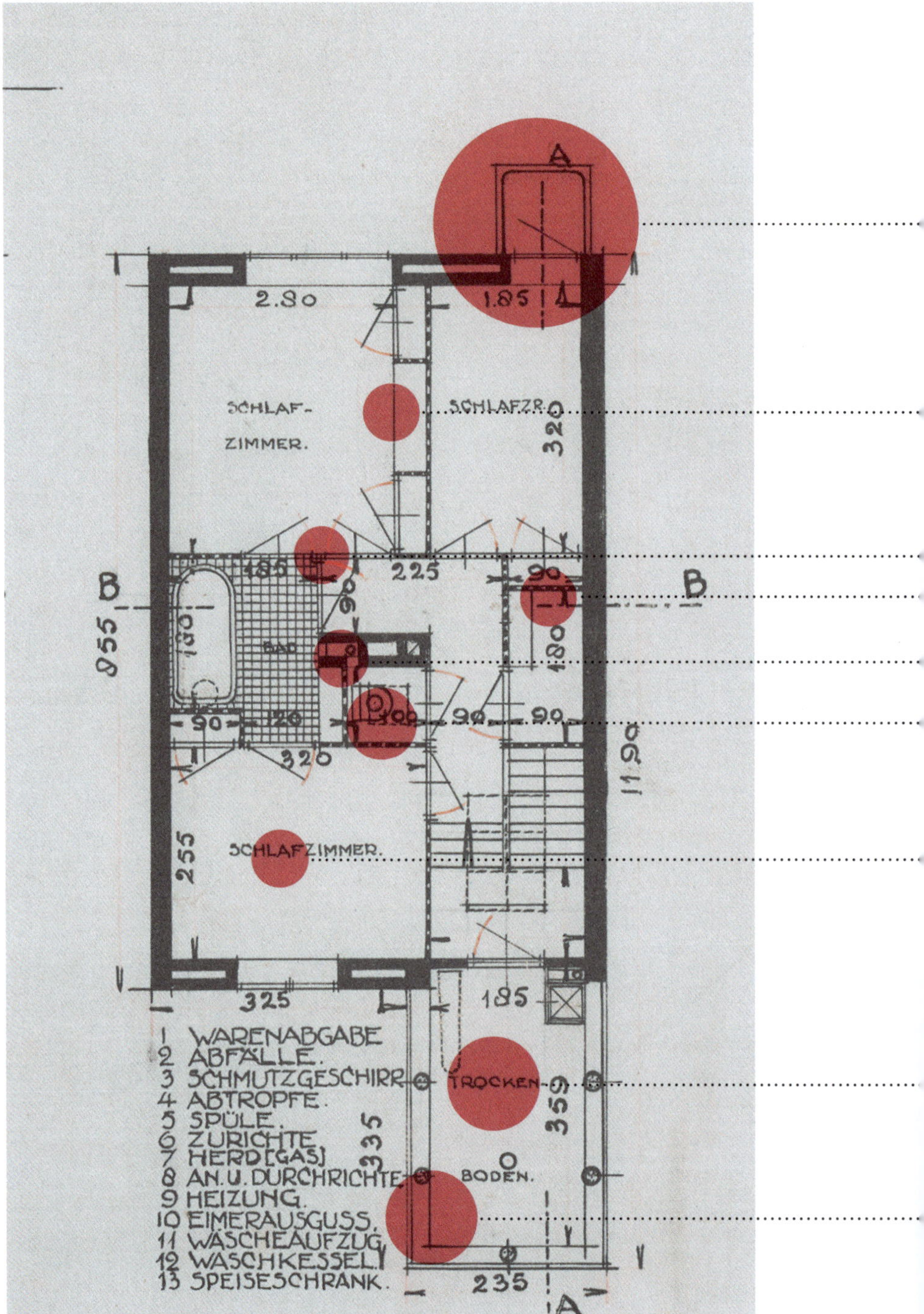
SCHLAF-
ZIMMER.
SCHLAFZR.
BAD
SCHLAFZIMMER.
TROCKEN-
BODEN.
1 WARENABGABE
2 ABFÄLLE.
3 SCHMUTZGESCHIRR
4 ABTROPFE.
5 SPÜLE.
6 ZURICHTE.
7 HERD[GAS]
8 AN.U.DURCHRICHTE
9 HEIZUNG.
10 EIMERAUSGUSS.
11 WÄSCHEAUFZUG.
12 WASCHKESSEL.
13 SPEISESCHRANK.

◀ An upper-level plan with annotations referencing Mr. Fassbaender's memories. **[33]**

Balcony off Rolf's bedroom, where he would drag the head of his mattress to sleep under the stars in the summer (figs. 24, 55–59)

Built-in makeup table in Rolf's mother's room; Mr. Fassbaender remembered this detail while walking through the identical row house, even though the furniture and the wall had been removed over time in that unit

Idiosyncratic moment where three doors meet, similarly remembered by Mr. Fassbaender

Built-in linen closet and shoe storage, some of the amenities designed by Oud and recalled by Mr. Fassbaender on the walk-through of number 7 (fig. 51)

Heat vent, which Mr. Fassbaender remembers using to warm up after baths (fig. 52)

A lack of acoustic isolation meant one could hear the toilet flush in all of the row houses

Lodger's room, often occupied by architecture students

Location of roof drain above in the laundry-drying room, where a ball once got stuck and caused a flood (figs. 53, 54)

Windows in the laundry-drying room from which Rolf would look down on the street and play pranks on friends (figs. 53, 54)

3

3
5

◀◀ The street-side service entrance to "number 3," where Rolf Fassbaender lived from 1927 to 1939, photographed in 2015. [34]
◀◀ Pankokweg, one of the streets in the Weissenhofsiedlung that the children claimed as their playground. [35]

▲ The Mies van der Rohe apartment building, whose stairwells were a good place for hiding or setting off firecrackers, and the small hill for sledding in front. [36]
▶ The location of the streetlight (no longer existing) Rolf shot out with his pellet gun on Pankokweg. [37]

◄◄ The low wall where the children counted while playing hide-and-seek, to the west of the Oud row houses. **[38]**

▲ The north side of the row houses, from Pankokweg. **[39]**

► The north (service) entrance to Rolf Fassbaender's childhood home. **[40]**

◄ The sheltered, street-side courtyard where Rolf's rabbits lived; they were brought to the front garden on sunny days. This photograph was taken at Pankokweg 7, a row house identical to Rolf's home at Pankokweg 3. **[41]**

▲ The view from a row house kitchen. The collaboration between J. J. P. Oud and Erna Meyer has made the kitchen a subject of significant scholarly attention, but it plays only a small role in Mr. Fassbaender's memories of the house. **[42]**

►► Windows from the service courtyard to the kitchen and entryway. [43]

▲ The path to the south (garden) side of the row houses. Access to the path had to be restricted to protect the inhabitants' privacy from onlookers, who continued to visit the avant-garde settlement after the exhibition. **[44]**

► The entrance to the row house with balcony off of Rolf's bedroom above. At the time "number 3" was the only garden with a tree—significant because "it was important to go up." **[45]**

►► The gardens "on the sunny side," where Rolf played with his friends and the rabbits. **[46]**

◄◄ The built-in concrete bench at Pankokweg 7, identical to where Rolf was sitting when a bird ate the butter off his bread. **[47]**

◄ The front door on the garden side. **[48]**
▲ Inside the entry vestibule was a built-in utility closet, which included a water tap for the garden. The interior photographs were taken in Pankokweg 7, a row house identical to Pankokweg 3, where Mr. Fassbaender grew up. **[49]**

◄◄ The windows facing the garden in the living room, where the "Tischrunde Fassbaender" took place: neighbors gathering in the evenings at the round table to share food and conversation. **[50]**

▲ The stair landing at the bedroom level, where Mr. Fassbaender remembers built-in cabinets for linen and shoe storage. **[51]**

► The bathroom. Mr. Fassbaender recalls a heat vent that he would stand near to warm up after baths. **[52]**

◄ Mr. Fassbaender remembers looking down from the laundry-drying room to the playground—the street. He would play pranks on his friends by calling out to them and then hiding from view. **[53]**

▲ Mr. Fassbaender recalls that a tennis ball once got stuck in the roof drain and caused a flood in the laundry-drying room. The water rose so high that it lifted up a dresser. **[54]**

▲ The smallest bedroom in the row house was occupied by Rolf. **[55]**

► The child's bedroom was the only one with a balcony. **[56]**

▲▶ As a boy, Rolf would drag the head of his mattress onto the balcony so he could sleep under the stars. **[57, 58]**

▶▶ The sunny gardens on the south of the row houses seen from the balcony. **[59]**

Notes

1 Richard Pommer and Christian F. Otto argue that the event's influence extended beyond architectural debates directly into society and politics: "The establishment of the International Style ... consolidated the opponents to the Modern Movement and drove them closer to the Right. Their reaction found justification in the double connotations of the term 'international' in Germany, where it implied not only the links between nations, but an absence of patriotic feeling—for the Left a virtue, for the Right a reproach." *Weissenhof 1927 and the Modern Movement in Architecture* (Chicago: University of Chicago Press, 1991), 164.

2 Ed Taverne, Cor Wagenaar, and Martien de Vletter describe the long engagement between Oud and the organizers of the exhibition, including the correspondence between Oud and Mies in planning the event as well as public lectures and newspaper articles authored by Oud in Stuttgart in anticipation of the event, in "Five Row Houses in the Weissenhofsiedlung," in *J. J. P. Oud: Poetic Functionalist, 1890–1963; The Complete Works* (Rotterdam: NAi Publishers, 2001), 290–303.

3 Pommer and Otto, *Weissenhof 1927*, 121–22. Anja Krämer explains further: "Oud was invited to design houses for workers and simple employees and his houses were seen as workmen houses at the time, especially in comparison with the other houses. They were the smallest houses with only 70 square meters. The other single family houses of the Estate had 110 to 150 square meters. But Pommer and Otto are also right, they are big for a worker house and tend to [be considered] middle class houses." Email correspondence with author, August 18, 2020.

4 Taverne et al., *J. J. P. Oud*, 294. See also Nicholas Bullock, "First the Kitchen: Then the Façade," *Journal of Design History* 1, no. 3/4 (1988): 177–92.

5 Taverne et al., *J. J. P. Oud*, 297.

6 See Richard Pommer, "The Flat Roof: A Modernist Controversy in Germany," *Art Journal* 43, no. 2, "Revising Modernist History: The Architecture of the 1920s and 1930s" (Summer 1983): 158–69; and William Rollins, "A Nation in White: Germany's Hygienic Consensus and the Ambiguities of Modernist Architecture," *German Politics & Society* 19, no. 4 (Winter 2001): 1–42.

7 Taverne et al., *J. J. P. Oud*, 34.

8 Henry-Russell Hitchcock Jr. and Philip Johnson, *The International Style: Architecture since 1922* (New York: W. W. Norton, 1932), 33. While the Museum of Modern Art exhibition was titled *Modern Architecture: International Exhibition*, the catalogue was republished as *The International Style: Architecture since 1922*.

9 James M. Markham, "In Stuttgart, Renovation of a 1927 Bauhaus Project," *New York Times*, May 17, 1984.

10 Anja Krämer explains: "In the neighborhood there existed a farm house, that belonged in the 18th century to a family named 'Weiss'. Later on, in the 19th century this farm became a popular restaurant destination in the outskirts of Stuttgart and it was named 'Weissenhof-Bäck' after the name of the family.

After this building and restaurant the area was named 'Am Weissenhof'." Email correspondence with author, April 17, 2020.

11 Taverne et al., *J. J. P. Oud*, 294.

12 Hitchcock and Johnson state that the balconies "lighten the design and give interest to the regular scheme." *International Style*, 199.

13 These plans changed with the early successes of the war, and the military command center was built on former French soil, in Strasbourg, instead. However, the Allied bombing campaign would go on to destroy nearly half the buildings at the Weissenhofsiedlung by the end of World War II.

14 Some, like the musician Mr. Busch, emigrated to Switzerland, while the policeman emigrated to Brazil. We know from Hans Reif that his family emigrated to the United States.

Tugendhat House

Ludwig Mies van der Rohe
Brno, Czech Republic
1930

The Tugendhat House, completed in 1930, was one of the most iconic buildings of the International Style[1] and "one of the most uncompromising statements of new architecture" of the early twentieth century.[2] Ludwig Mies van der Rohe received the commission from Grete Tugendhat (née Löw-Beer) and her husband, Fritz, in 1928, after Grete's parents gave her a plot of land in the Černá Pole district of Brno and the funds to construct a new home as a wedding gift. As Alice Rawsthorn notes, "The Tugendhats ... were wonderfully accommodating clients who had told Mies precisely what they needed from their home, then given him carte blanche and a seemingly limitless budget to build it."[3]

The house is a *Gesamtkunstwerk*, a total work of art, with every detail considered by the architect and his team of designers and craftsmen, which included the interior designer Lilly Reich and the landscape architect Grete Roder-Müller.[4] From its careful siting on the hill overlooking medieval Brno to the interior spatial configurations (living room windows that lower into the floor, the placement of custom furniture) to the textures and colors of the fabrics and even the detailing of the door handles, the building is a complete vision of luxurious Modernist living.[5]

The upper, street level of the house consists of an ample entrance hall and a series of cellular bedrooms; a grand, open living area makes up the garden level below. The villa also accommodates a large service wing, which includes a garage and servant quarters. With these divisions, as Wolf Tegethoff argues, "the general disposition of the house continued to represent 19th century upper-class social habits and ideals."[6]

It is the main level of the house that exemplifies the free planning principles Mies espoused. The fluid space is defined by opulent partitions in onyx and zebrawood and formal furniture configurations,[7] both intentionally independent of the grid of structural columns. The design emphasizes "spatial relationships rather than built forms," Christian Norberg-Schulz writes. "Overlooking the landscape through the continuous and mobile glass wall, the living zone expresses a 'freedom' unknown in any previous dwelling."[8]

Over the years, the house has had many functions. After the Tugendhats, who were Jewish, fled the house in 1938 in advance of the Nazi occupation, it served as an army barracks and horse stable, first for the Germans and then for the Red Army.

In Communist times, it was a children's rehabilitation center and dance school. In 1992, the declaration that dissolved Czechoslovakia was signed in the house. At present it is a museum.

Beginning in 2010, the Tugendhat House underwent an extensive, two-year renovation meant to restore Mies's design; as Carsten Krohn asserts, "The original condition has been so exactingly reconstructed that it is now hard to tell what is original and what is reconstruction."[9] While experts question certain details, such as the verisimilitude of the colors of the furnishings,[10] others have criticized the result in more conceptual terms: "In Tugendhat, every trace of the violent and tragic history of this house since 1928 has been erased with a manic precision never witnessed before," Wouter Vanstiphout writes. "The absence of history has ... created a haunted house, shimmering and throbbing with memories forever out of reach."[11]

◀ The Tugendhat House photographed from the garden shortly after its completion, circa 1930/31. **[1]**

◀ The house seen from Černopolní Street. **[2]**

▼ An exterior view of the house showing its relationship to the hill. **[3]**

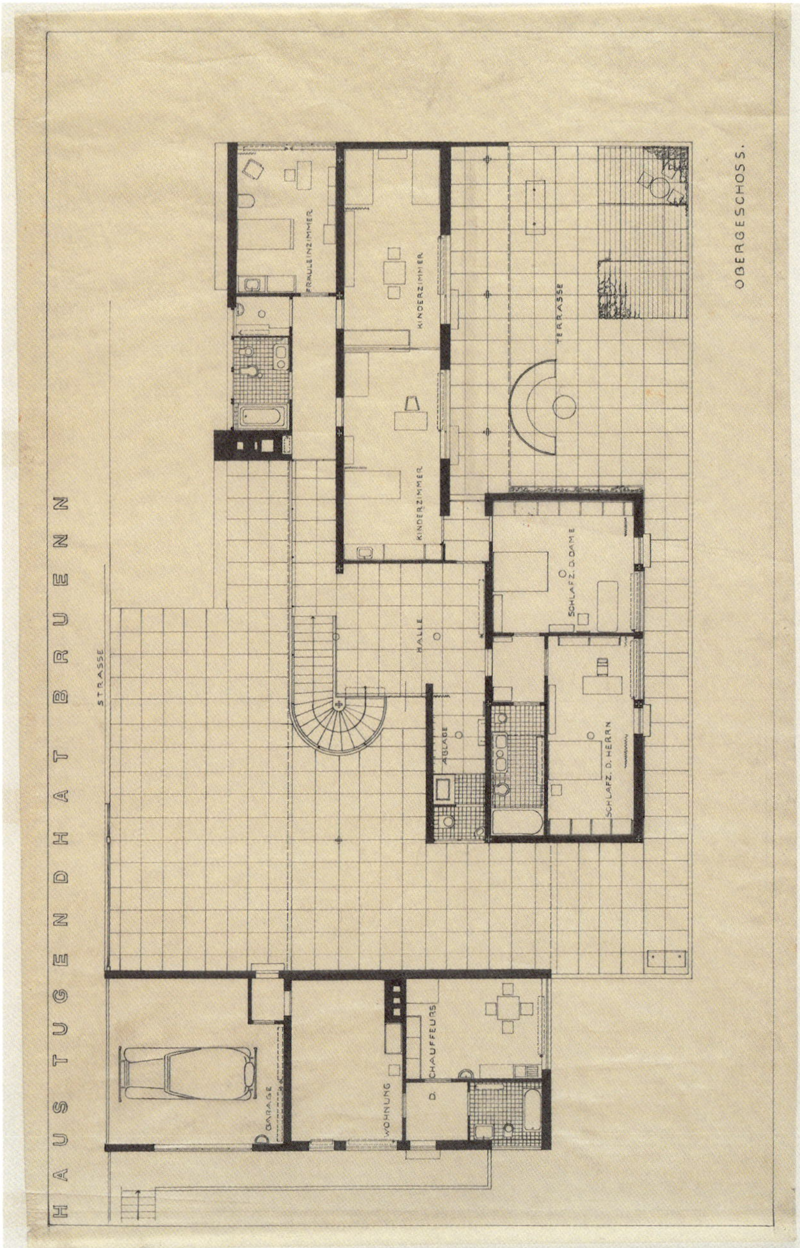

▲ A street-level (upstairs) plan by Ludwig Mies van der Rohe, 1928–30. [4]

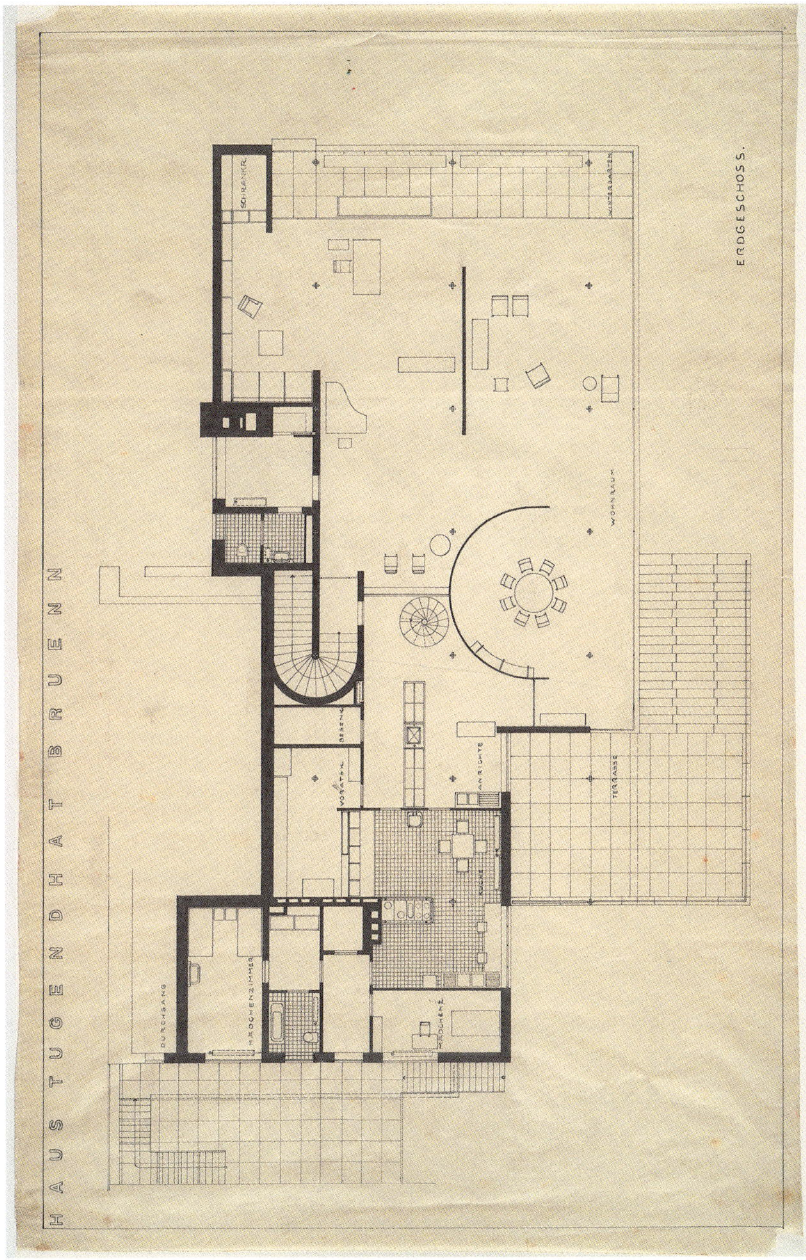

▲ A main-level plan by Ludwig Mies van der Rohe, 1928–30. [5]

Conversation with Ernst Tugendhat

Ernst Tugendhat, a philosopher and retired professor of philosophy, is the only surviving member of the Tugendhat family who lived in the famous house in Brno.[12] Ernst was born in March 1930; the family moved into the building in December of the same year. He was only eight years old when the family abandoned the house, fleeing the imminent Nazi occupation of Czechoslovakia. He does not have strong ties to the building: "I'm relatively neutral to the house. It didn't matter to me so much."[13]

In the time the family lived in the house, Grete and Fritz Tugendhat had three children: Hanna, Grete's daughter from her previous marriage; Ernst; and Herbert, the youngest. There was also a large staff, which included a nanny, a chauffeur (whose wife and dog also lived in the house), a cook, and two maids.

Mr. Tugendhat's recollections of his childhood dwelling are incomplete; only a handful of episodes figure strongly in his mind. "I'm very old. I'm 85. ... I don't remember much of my life," he said when we met. He is conscious that the numerous photographs his father took of the home are a record of his time there, but they don't trigger memories (fig. 7).[14] "Really, my conscious life began in the three years in Switzerland," where the family first lived after fleeing Brno, he explained. During our interview, he also recognized how his own recollections have been altered over time: "I have seen the house a few times now in the last years," he said. "What I remember of the house is what I saw when I visited the house again, [rather] than from my childhood."

Asked to describe the Tugendhat House, he responded, smiling, "It was impressive." The living room's onyx wall and the moveable windows stand out in his mind (figs. 8–10, 53), as did the division of the upstairs "dormitories." "We had separate rooms. The children were in one section and the parents in another section," he recalled, though he did not remember how the two zones were joined. The remark is notable, as Ernst's room had a dedicated shortcut to his mother's bedroom via additional doors and a connecting vestibule, a feature specifically requested by Grete Tugendhat after reviewing Mies's plans for the house for the first time (figs. 37, 38).[15]

The boys shared a bedroom (figs. 34–37), while their sister Hanna had her own (figs. 41, 42). It was in these rooms that the children ate their dinner with the nanny, Irene Kalkofen.[16] The caregiver had her own room close to those of the children.[17] The children ate their lunch in the main dining area downstairs, "at the round table" (figs. 54, 55). "I was thinking about it before you came now: I don't really know how much we were downstairs in the large room, but we were quite often. But in the evening, we were always upstairs," he reflected.

Mr. Tugendhat doesn't recall any particular feelings toward specific spaces in the house—for example, rooms where he felt comfortable or safe, or where he spent the most time. "I don't think I had a favorite place," he said. In contrast, he retains a certain attachment to the furniture of the house, as he was able to spend more time with it over the years. "We were very lucky because a large part of our furniture from the Brno house was sent by my father to St. Gallen, where we lived for three years," he explained. "And then from St. Gallen we moved in 1941, which was a very dangerous time, to Venezuela, and again we had a whole container, and

◄ Ernst Tugendhat photographed in his apartment in Freiburg, 2015. [6]

▲ Ernst reaching for the upper-level entrance door handle. [7]

it arrived in Venezuela—which was really surprising! So, a large part of the furniture of the house went to St. Gallen first and then to Venezuela and later back into Switzerland again. My sisters have quite a few of the furniture pieces" (figs. 11, 49, 50). The white leather Brno library chairs and the tan leather Tugendhat chair "were with us all the way in Switzerland and Venezuela afterwards, so therefore to these chairs ... I have much more of a relationship than to the house itself," he said, prompted by a photograph (fig. 12).

Mr. Tugendhat's strongest memories are associated with the outdoor spaces of the house, which left a significant emotional mark; however, these memories have little to do with the architectural setting and more to do with the circumstances

▲ The living room windows that could retract into the basement, seen from inside and outside. **[8, 9]**

▲ The study and living areas, separated by the onyx wall. [10]
▼ The library, with white leather Brno chairs designed by Mies and Lilly Reich. [11]

(figs. 13, 19, 20, 56–61). The first is associated with the garden: "One incident ... was with the tortoise, which was a very disagreeable but very strong memory. We had two or three tortoises and the one was somehow off somewhere and I took it—I was six years old—and I threw it back. It fell precisely on a stone, and the back was bleeding on the shell, so it had to be killed." Mr. Tugendhat grimaced with discomfort in relaying the memory. "I had very strong feelings with animals," he said.

The second episode took place on the street and also involved animals (figs. 26–28). "In the terrace in front of the house there was a carriage ... and the man whipped the horses, and I was completely terrified," he said. "I wept and ran back into the house. I couldn't see it anymore."

A more joyful memory he shared was of playing and hearing the car horn—a distinctive "da-da-dada" sound—signaling his father's arrival home. He also remembers playing with a child-sized car on the upper terrace, the "platform," where there was a sandbox, a pergola, and a built-in bench (figs. 14–16, 29–33).

▼ Hanna and Ernst (right) reading on the tan leather Tugendhat chair in the library. **[12]**

Mr. Tugendhat did not recall any particular rules or restrictions in the way that the children were allowed to use the house. Of the onyx wall in particular, he said that his parents "certainly considered it precious, but [it] was not vulnerable, so there was no reason to tell the children not to touch it" (figs. 17, 53). At the same time, he does not think the building encouraged creativity, play, or freedom in the children. "I think it was a certain feeling one couldn't change things so much [in the house]," he reflected. He recounted a story about the piano in the nanny's room, which had not been part of Mies's layout, and which the family moved to the basement when they found out that the architect was coming for a visit.[18] The visit did not materialize, but so strict was the architect about the execution and maintenance of his design intent that the inhabitants inherited the ethos. "This story doesn't affect me in any way, but it shows somehow what the spirit was," he explained. However, he does not believe that his parents felt constrained by the

▼ One of Fritz Tugendhat's photographs of the house, showing the lush garden once the landscape had matured. **[13]**

▲ The children on the children's terrace, which Mr. Tugendhat called the "platform," with the pergola to the right and the sandbox beyond. **[14]**
▼ From left: the walkway leading to the children's terrace; the rounded bench outside Ernst and Herbert's room. **[15, 16]**

▲ The open living room, with onyx wall, looking toward the winter garden. **[17]**
▶ The winter garden. **[18]**

architect's orders or prescriptions: "My parents wrote letters to a magazine because of the question of how they felt about the house. And they didn't consider their freedom relinquished."[19]

In Mr. Tugendhat's view, living in the house had little effect on his identity and did not influence his dwelling preferences later on: "It was quite unimportant for me where I lived. I'm a philosopher," he stated. He described to us his different living situations over the years: "When I went to Stanford, I first lived in a dorm for two years. I think this shows the little significance the living situation had for me, that I took an extremely small room and I was very happy to find a room again where I didn't have a roommate." From student dormitories to a "normal apartment" in

Tübingen and "quite a nice place in Berlin," which "was more or less a coincidence," he said that his homes have mattered little to him over his lifetime. The apartment on the second floor of a house where he lives now, and where we met, is also spacious and tastefully furnished, but Mr. Tugendhat asserted that this is entirely the purview of the landlord, as she had the house built and the furniture belongs to her (figs. 21, 22).

While Mr. Tugendhat agreed that Mies likely thought that architecture could improve inhabitants' lives, he does not believe so himself. "If I would have become an adult in that house, I don't think I would have stayed, because of what I call ... what was my word? Embarrassment," he said. "I find it strange that my parents built a house like this. But when I was eight years old, I didn't reflect on this point. I think if I would have stayed longer, I would have felt embarrassed to live in such a palace[-like] house." He emphasized that he doesn't understand why his parents

◀ A view of the house from the garden below. **[19]**

▲ The southwest facade, looking into the winter garden through the trees. **[20]**

"built a thing so pompous" in a "town like Brno." "I find it strange that my parents went to Mies van der Rohe and asked him to build a house for them. They talked with Mies and finally he sent them these plans and they were a bit surprised that it was much larger than what they had thought of. But they didn't have this feeling of embarrassment which I would have had," he added.

Over the course of our conversation, which was quite personal, Mr. Tugendhat apologized repeatedly for how little he remembers: "I'm sorry that I have so little. The life that I remember began later." "I feel very sympathetic to your questions, the way you do it, I didn't expect this at all," he said at the end of the interview. "I didn't expect that you would have such a subjective interest in the subject. … I thought you were more interested in knowing something positive about the house."

▲ Views of Mr. Tugendhat's apartment, 2015. The apartment was furnished by his landlord. **[21, 22]**

► Stills from Ernst Tugendhat's conversation with the authors, 2015. **[23]**

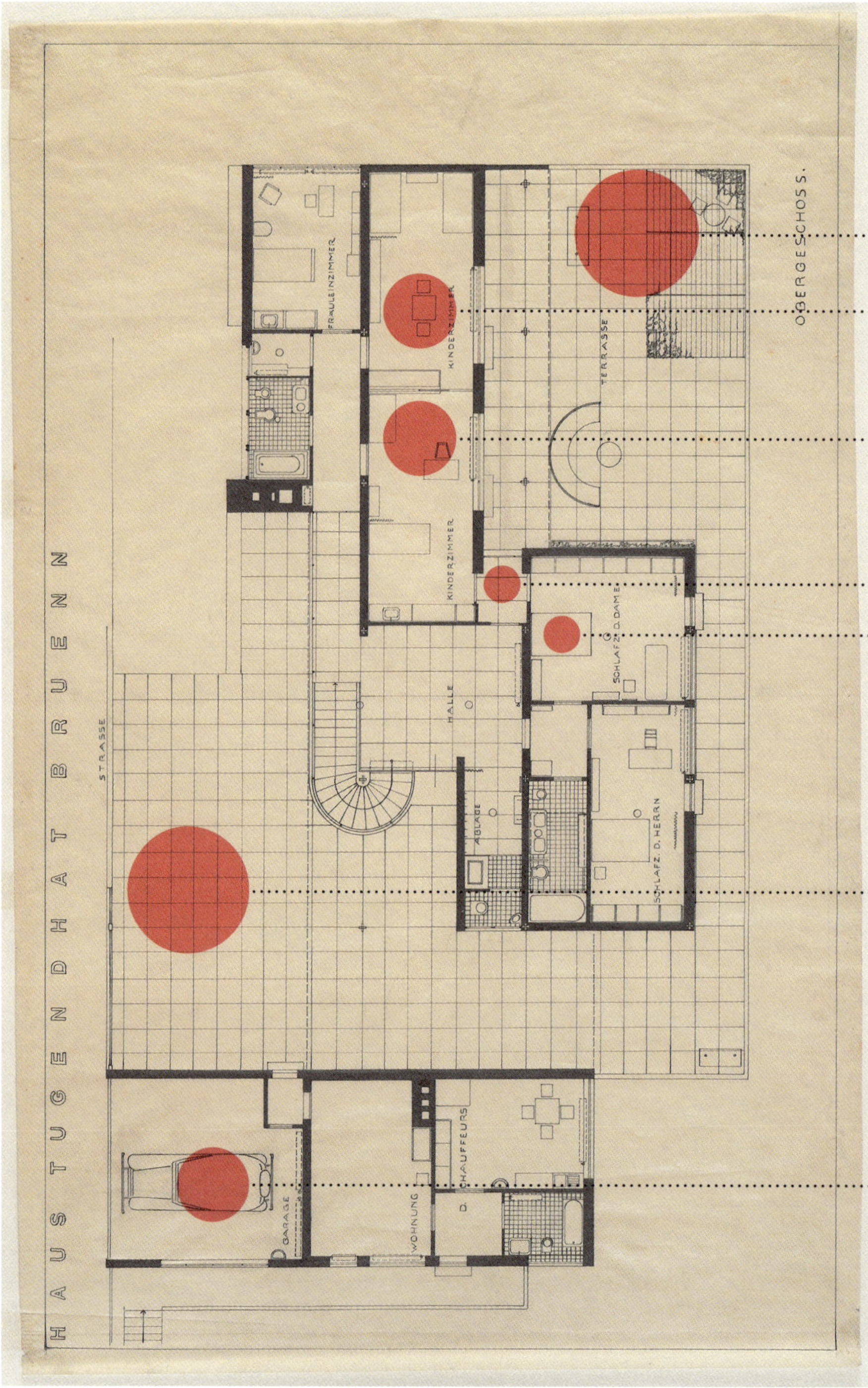
HAUS TUGENDHAT BRUENN
OBERGESCHOSS.
FRÄULEINZIMMER
KINDERZIMMER
KINDERZIMMER
TERRASSE
SCHLAFZ. D. DAME
SCHLAFZ. D. HERRN
HALLE
ABLAGE
STRASSE
GARAGE
WOHNUNG
CHAUFFEURS
D.

◄ A street-level plan with annotations referencing Mr. Tugendhat's memories. [24]

Children's terrace, which Mr. Ernst Tugendhat called the "platform," where he played with his siblings in the sandbox and with a toy car (figs. 14–16, 29–33)

Ernst's sister Hanna's bedroom: the children ate their evening meal here or in the boys' nursery with their nanny (figs. 41, 42)

Boys' nursery, shared by Ernst with his younger brother Herbert (figs. 34–37)

Passage doors and vestibule between the boys' room and that of their mother, a connection Grete Tugendhat requested upon seeing the plans for the house for the first time (fig. 38)

Grete Tugendhat's bedroom (fig. 38)

Forecourt, where Mr. Tugendhat remembers witnessing a man with a horse-drawn carriage whipping his horses on the street, one of the strongest memories he has from living in the house (figs. 26–28)

Garage; Mr. Tugendhat remembers listening for the distinctive "da-da-dada" sound of the car horn signaling the arrival home of his father

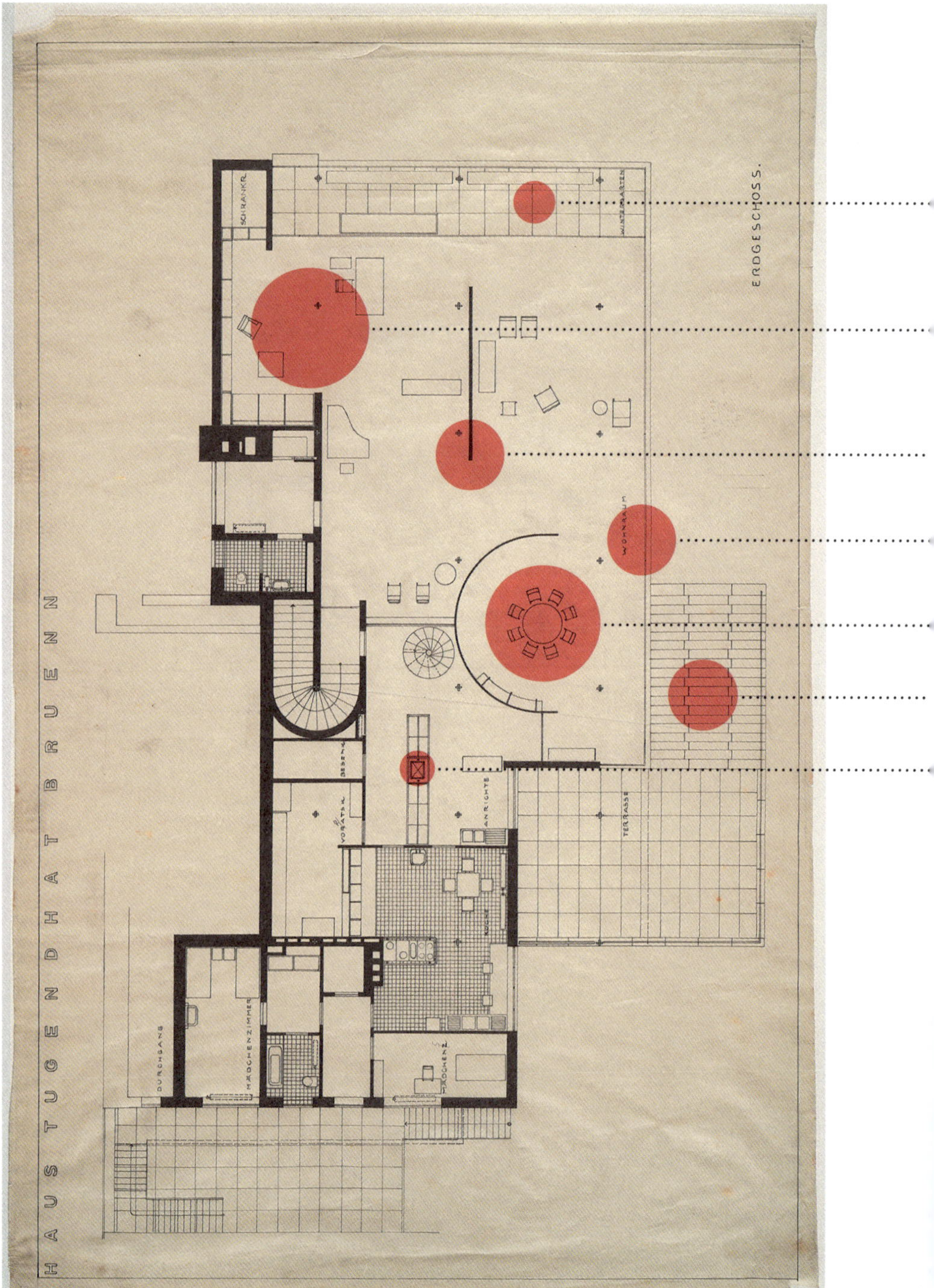
HAUS TUGENDHAT BRUENN
ERDGESCHOSS.
SCHRANKR.
WINTERGARTEN
WOHNRAUM
TERRASSE
ANRICHTE
KÜCHE
KÖCHENZ.
MÄDCHENZIMMER
DURCHGANG
VORRÄTE
BESEN

◀ A main-level plan with annotations referencing Mr. Tugendhat's memories. **[25]**

.... Winter garden, one of the most idiosyncratic spaces of the house (figs. 18, 52). While there are photographs of Ernst as a small child in the winter garden, he does not have any childhood memories of the space

.... The chairs, including the Mies-designed white leather Brno library chairs and the tan leather Tugendhat chair, are dear to Mr. Tugendhat, as the family was able to take them into exile: "I have much more of a relationship [to the chairs] than to the house itself" (figs. 11, 12, 49, 50)

.... Onyx wall; though his parents certainly considered it precious, "the onyx wall was not vulnerable, so there was no reason to tell the children not to touch it," according to Mr. Tugendhat (figs. 10, 17, 53)

.... Windows that could retract into the basement below, one of the most characteristic elements of the house and one remembered by Mr. Tugendhat (figs. 8, 9, 51)

.... Round table, where the children ate their lunch (figs. 54, 55)

.... Steps leading down to the garden below, where Mr. Tugendhat remembers playing and where he has a strong memory of accidentally injuring one of the family's tortoises (figs. 13, 56, 57)

.... Dumbwaiter, used to deliver the children's evening meal upstairs (fig. 46)

◀◀ The entry of the Tugendhat House from Černopolní Street, with Brno in the background, photographed in 2015. Ernst Tugendhat lived here from 1930 to 1938. **[26]**

▲ The main entrance is concealed by a curving glass volume. **[27]**
▶ The forecourt, where Mr. Tugendhat remembers witnessing a man with a horse-drawn carriage whipping his horses on the street. This is one of his strongest memories of living in the home. The incident terrified the child: "I wept and ran back into the house. I couldn't see it anymore." **[28]**

◀ The walkway in front of Ernst's parents' bedrooms leading to the children's terrace. The children would ride their bicycles and toy cars here. **[29]**

▲ The children's terrace (the "platform"), with semi-circular bench and pergola. **[30]**

◄◄ The sandbox on the terrace. Mr. Tugendhat remembers listening for the distinctive "da-da-dada" sound of the car horn signaling his father's arrival home from work. **[31]**

▲ The planted pergola and a view from the terrace to Brno beyond. **[32]**

► The children's bedrooms had windows and doors leading directly onto the terrace. **[33]**

◄◄ The boys' nursery, with Ernst's bed against the wall. Though not among the furniture designed by Mies van der Rohe and his team, these pieces, like most furniture in the house, were recreated as part of the extensive 2012 restoration of the house. **[34]**

▲ The view and access to the terrace from the nursery. The door to the left opens directly into Ernst's sister Hanna's bedroom. The children ate their evening meal in the nursery or in Hanna's room next door. **[35]**

► The crib of Ernst's younger brother Herbert, with storage cabinets and built-in basin beyond. **[36]**

◄ The door connecting the nursery directly to the bedroom of Ernst's mother, Grete, via a small vestibule. This shortcut does not figure in Mr. Tugendhat's memory; he recalls instead the greater distance between the regular entrances to the bedrooms, which were separated by a corridor and the entry hall. **[37]**

▲ Grete Tugendhat's bedroom. To the right is the small vestibule that connects to the boys' bedroom. Grete requested this link upon seeing the plans for the house for the first time. **[38]**

◀ The children's bathroom. **[39]**

▲ The double sink in the children's bathroom. **[40]**

◄ The bedroom of Ernst's older sister, Hanna. **[41]**

▲ The table in Hanna's room where the nanny, Irene Kalkofen, sometimes served the children's evening meal. **[42]**

▲ The generous entrance hall connecting the entryway to the bedrooms and the living spaces downstairs. Ernst can be seen reaching for the entrance door handle in fig. 7. **[43]**
▶ The stair connecting the two levels of the house. **[44]**

◄ The service spaces, including the access to the kitchen and a stair leading to the basement. **[45]**

▲ The dumbwaiter that was used to deliver the children's evening meal upstairs. **[46]**

◀ The entry into the main living space downstairs. "I don't really know how much we were downstairs in the large room, but we were quite often. But in the evening, we were always upstairs," Mr. Tugendhat recalled. **[47]**

▲ A view of the writing desk in the study, with the winter garden beyond. **[48]**

▲ The writing desk and the library beyond. [49]
▶ The family was able to take much of the furniture with them when they fled from the Nazis, first to Switzerland, then to Venezuela, and later back to Switzerland. For that reason, the chairs, such as the white leather Brno library chairs and the tan leather Tugendhat chair designed by Mies and Lilly Reich (see fig. 49), are dear to Mr. Tugendhat: "I have much more of a relationship [to the chairs] than to the house itself." [50]

◄◄ A view into the main seating area, with the winter garden beyond and the garden to the right. The windows could be completely retracted into the basement to heighten continuity between the inside and outside. [51]

◄ While there are photographs of Ernst as a small child in the winter garden, he does not have any childhood memories of the space. [52]

▲ Mr. Tugendhat remembers the onyx wall. Though his parents certainly considered it precious, "the onyx wall was not vulnerable, so there was no reason to tell the children not to touch it." [53]

▲ The children ate lunch with their parents "at the round table," screened by the semi-circular partition. [54]

▶ The circular table could be configured for large gatherings, as shown here, but its perimeter leaves could also be removed to accommodate more intimate meals. [55]

▲ The steps leading to the garden below. **[56]**

► The basement level of the house, seen here behind the vine-covered wall, contained service areas as well as the darkroom of Fritz Tugendhat, a passionate photographer. **[57]**

►► The house seen from the garden below. Mr. Tugendhat's strongest memories of the house are of the exterior spaces. **[58]**

◄ The stratification of the levels of the house: the garden, the living spaces (with the onyx wall visible), and the children's terrace. **[59]**

▲ One of Mr. Tugendhat's memories from living in the house involves the garden. He remembers throwing one of the family's pet tortoises back toward the garden after it had wandered off. The animal's shell accidentally hit a stone, and it had to be killed: "a very disagreeable but very strong memory." **[60]**

►► Mr. Tugendhat is indifferent to the famous house he grew up in, but he also has very few memories of the years he lived there. Most of his conscious memories start at the age of eight, from the time when his family lived in St. Gallen, Switzerland, after they fled the Nazis. **[61]**

Notes

1 Photographs and a model of the building were featured in the Museum of Modern Art's *Modern Architecture: International Exhibition* in 1932; see pages 116–17 of the associated exhibition catalogue, https://www.moma.org/documents/moma_catalogue_2044_300061855.pdf.

2 Arthur Drexler, *Ludwig Mies van der Rohe* (New York: George Braziller, 1960), 21.

3 Alice Rawsthorn, "Reopening a Mies Modernist Landmark," *New York Times,* February 24, 2012.

4 In particular, scholars have noted Reich's involvement with the fabrics and furnishings. See Marianne Eggler, "Divide and Conquer: Ludwig Mies van der Rohe and Lilly Reich's Fabric Partitions at the Tugendhat House," *Studies in the Decorative Arts* 16, no. 2 (Spring-Summer 2009): 66–90; and Robin Schuldenfrei, *Luxury and Modernism: Architecture and the Object in Germany 1900–1933* (Princeton, NJ: Princeton University Press, 2018).

5 "The room is a *Gesamtkunstwerk*: the house, its furniture and fittings are conceived as a whole. Mies not only designed a number of items of furniture for the house, including the Brno Chair and Brno Armchair, but also specified where they should stand. Even the round dining table is anchored to the floor." Carsten Krohn, *Mies van der Rohe: The Built Work* (Basel: Birkhäuser, 2014), 82. For a discussion of the luxurious materiality of the house, see Schuldenfrei, *Luxury and Modernism.*

6 "Mies, as well as Grete and Fritz Tugendhat, still belonged to a generation molded in the late Victorian age. This may explain why on the surface traditional concepts of living were still clung to; concepts which had long since ceased to be reconcilable with their intellectual way of thinking." Wolf Tegethoff, "The Tugendhat 'Villa': A Modern Residence in Turbulent Times," in Daniela Hammer-Tugendhat, Ivo Hammer, and Wolf Tegethoff, *Tugendhat House: Ludwig Mies van der Rohe*, new ed. (Basel: Birkhäuser, 2015), 129–30.

7 On Mies's use of high-end materials, see Schuldenfrei, *Luxury and Modernism*, 158: "Rather than using materials to express concepts of mass production, industry, or technology, as many of his peers did, Mies's materials were statements of modern elegance and luxury." On Mies's approach to furniture, Philip Johnson wrote, "No other important contemporary architect cares so much about placing furniture. Mies gives as much thought to placing chairs in a room as other architects do to placing buildings around a square." *Mies van der Rohe* (New York: Museum of Modern Art, 1947), 60.

8 Christian Norberg-Schulz, *Tugendhat House, Brno*, Architettura / Documenti, vol. 5 (Rome: Officina, 1984), 25, 21.

9 Krohn, *Mies van der Rohe,* 84.

10 "The aesthetic colour accents of the interior design, the 'emerald green' of the Tugendhat chairs and the 'ruby red' of the chaise longue are much too vibrant in the replicas." Ivo Hammer, "Materiality: History of the Tugendhat House 1997–2012; Conservation-Science Study and Restoration," in Hammer-Tugendhat et al., *Tugendhat House*, 221.

11 Wouter Vanstiphout, "The Most Ruthless Restoration in History," *Building Design* 2038 (November 23, 2012): 9.

12 Mr. Tugendhat was the hardest of our interlocutors to locate. We eventually received his address from the University of Tübingen, after contacting several members of the philosophy department there.

13 Mr. Tugendhat also shared this sentiment in an interview with Ulrike Herrmann: "That house never played a role in my life, or if it did, then it was a negative one. It's a matter of complete indifference to me where I live. Perhaps that's a reaction to our family's glorifying the house so much." Originally published as "Die Zeit des Philosophierens ist vorbei," *Die Tageszeitung*, July 28, 2007, https://taz.de/!253784/; translated as "The Time for Philosophising Is Over," signandsight.com, August 20, 2007, http://www.signandsight.com/features/1487.html.

14 When asked if he remembers anything about the winter garden in the house, for example, Mr. Tugendhat replied, pointing at historical photos, "No, practically. Only through these pictures." For the numerous photographs by Fritz Tugendhat of the family in the house, see Hammer-Tugendhat et al., *Tugendhat House*.

15 Grete Tugendhat, "On the Construction of the Tugendhat House," lecture, Brno House of Arts, January 17, 1969, printed and translated in Hammer-Tugendhat et al., *Tugendhat House*, 20.

16 For Irene Kalkofen's recollections of the house, see Hammer-Tugendhat et al., *Tugendhat House*, 84–89.

17 The nanny's room was also occasionally used as a guest room. During these times, Irene Kalkofen slept in the second bed in Hanna's room.

18 Several inhabitants, including Grete Tugendhat and Irene Kalkofen, recount this story in Hammer-Tugendhat et al., *Tugendhat House*, 52, 87.

19 Grete Tugendhat and Fritz Tugendhat, "The Inhabitants of the Tugendhat House Give Their Opinion," letter to the editor, *Die Form* 6, no. 11, November 15, 1931, reprinted and translated in Hammer-Tugendhat et al., *Tugendhat House*, 74–79.

Schminke House

Hans Scharoun
Löbau, Germany
1933

Historians have called the Schminke House "unrestrainedly modernist" and a "pioneering work of organic architecture."[1] The house coalesced Hans Scharoun's ideas and design methodologies related to domesticity and was the architect's final project before Nazi restrictions limited his freedom of formal experimentation.[2]

Fritz and Charlotte Schminke became acquainted with Scharoun's work at the 1929 Deutscher Werkbund–sponsored *Wohnung und Werkraum Ausstellung* (Living and Workspace Exhibition) in Breslau (now Wrocław, Poland). There they saw the Hostel for Unmarried Workers, a programmatically and architecturally innovative housing project designed by the architect, who was also a professor at the city's university.[3]

Unlike his contemporaries Walter Gropius and Ludwig Mies van der Rohe, who pursued a more rationalist design founded on structural logic and pure, orthogonal geometries,[4] Scharoun approached the Schminke House as an experiential sequence of spaces, or what J. Christoph Bürkle calls a "functional sequence."[5] "Despite its openness, this is not a general purpose flexible plan in the Miesian sense, but rather a series of dedicated rooms visually and spatially linked," Peter Blundell Jones states.[6] Accommodating the needs of the family through a series of interconnected rooms (figs. 4, 5), the Schminke House emerged from the "inside outwards,"[7] as it also adapted to the existing, stepped topography of the site.[8] As a result, the house appears grounded and embedded from the south and lighter, almost floating, to the north, where it faces the garden (figs. 1–3).[9]

Scharoun, who himself grew up in the port city of Bremerhaven, brought to the project a series of nautical references and structural techniques. These included not

only circular windows and patterns, but also, more fundamentally, a steel frame construction that allowed the house's particular openness and enabled its characteristic horizontal cantilevers. Scharoun's "pursuit of the ship-like was no mere affectation: it provided a radical alternative to the prevailing building culture both visually and technologically," Flora Samuel and Blundell Jones argue.[10]

A distinctive design aspect of the Schminke House is the 26-degree angle defined by the entry stairway and carried forward in the rotation of the winter garden and service area volumes that accentuate the extremities of the house (fig. 5). On the interior, the rotation enables a particular fluidity between spaces that extends out toward the garden. As Samuel and Blundell Jones explain, for Scharoun the Schminke House "marked the characteristic breakthrough in the use of free angles which has been his main legacy to late twentieth-century architecture."[11]

◄ The Schminke House photographed by Alice Kerling, 1933. [1]
▲ The protruding cantilevers of the terraces on the northeast facade. [2]
▼ The diagonal staircase negotiating the levels of the house and garden. [3]

Despite the relative lack of attention devoted to Scharoun in canonical architectural history,[12] the Schminke House remains one of the most singular and significant examples of Modernist domestic architecture. In its use of bold color, its sensitivity to site, and the experience of movement it enables, the house makes a unique and complex contribution to Modernism's legacy.

The family left the home in 1951, after which it became a clubhouse for the socialist youth movement Freie Deutsche Jugend (Free German Youth) and then an East German "Pioneer House." It was renovated and reopened as a museum in 2000.

▼ The open living spaces, with bespoke furnishings and lighting. **[4]**

▶ The double-height entry hall adjoining the children's playroom and the dining room. **[5]**

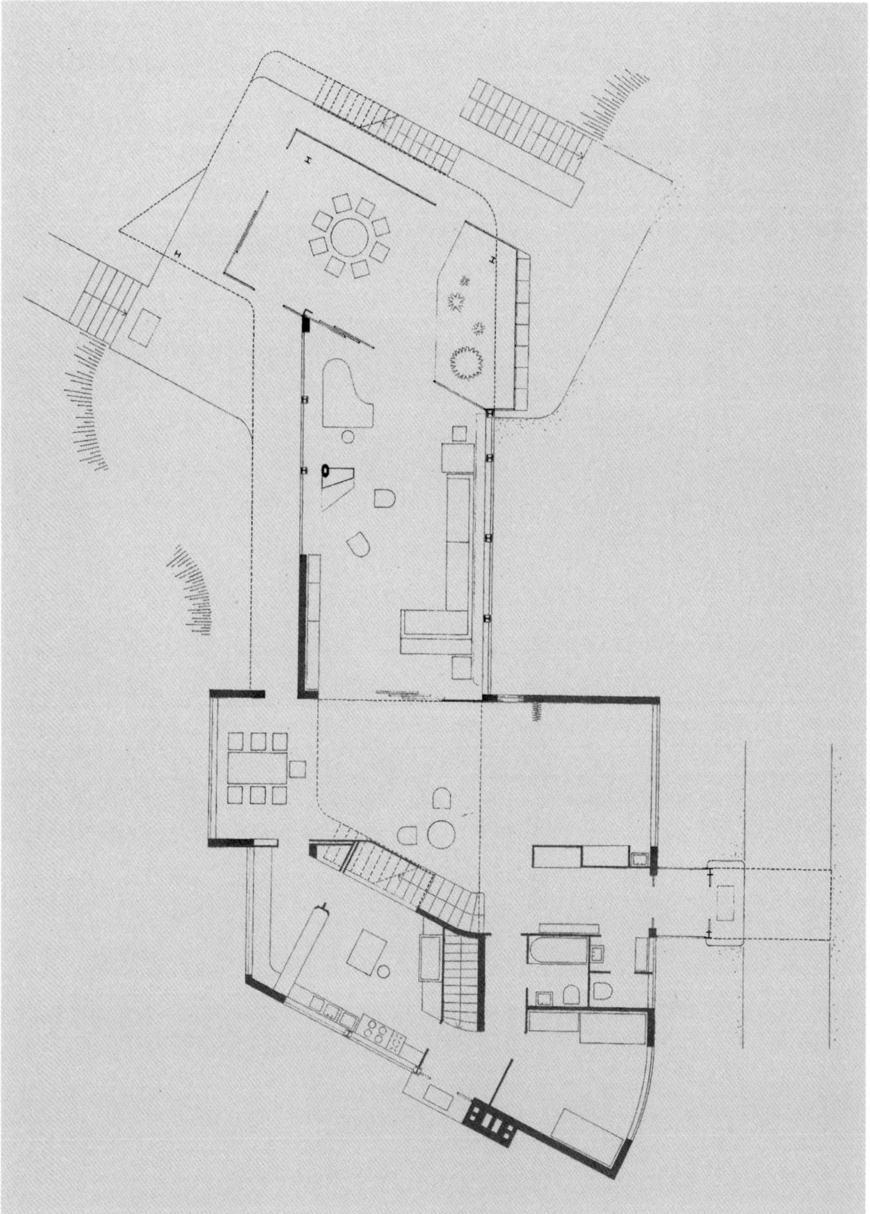

▲ A main-level plan of the Schminke House by Hans Scharoun. [6]

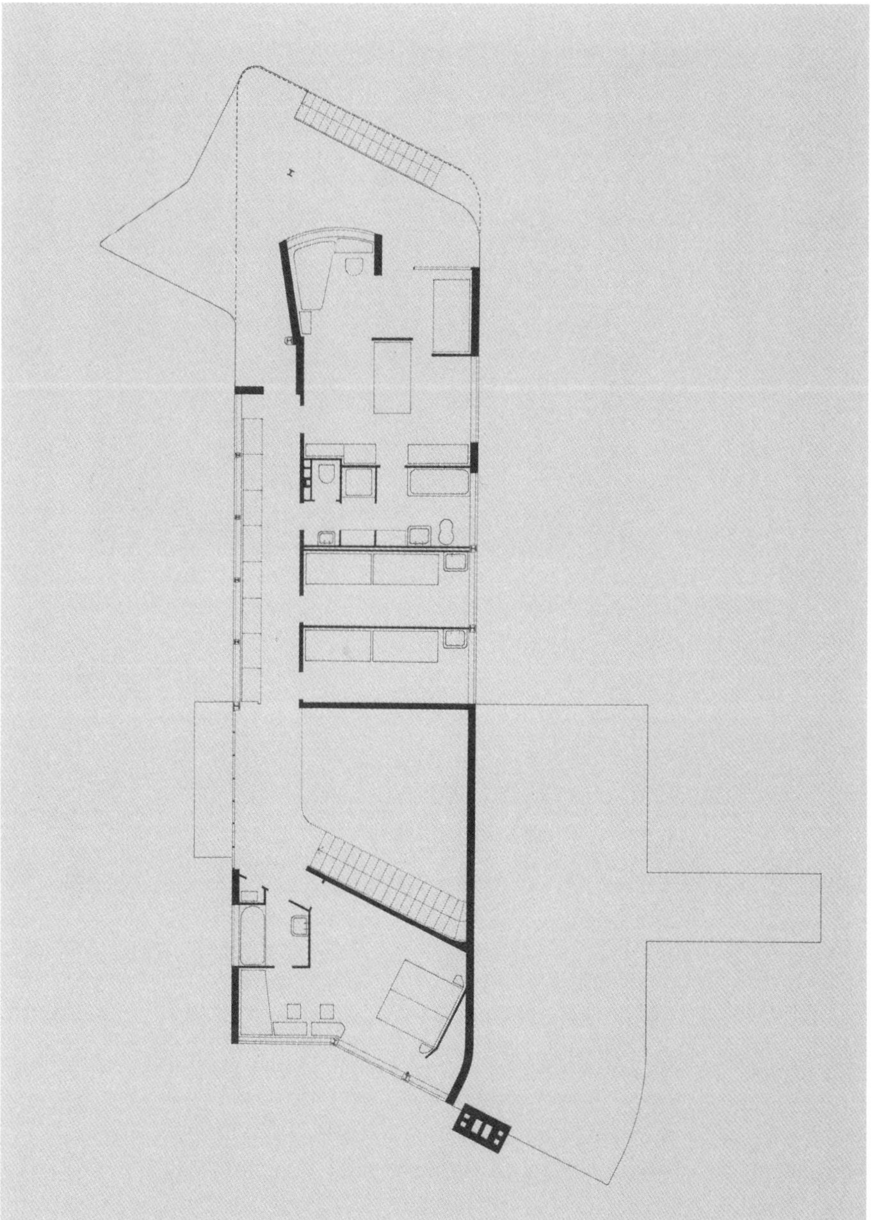

▲ An upper-level plan of the Schminke House by Hans Scharoun. [7]

Conversation with
Helga Zumpfe

Helga Zumpfe, née Schminke, was nearly three years old when her family of six moved into the Schminke House on May 31, 1933. In total, she lived in the dwelling for fifteen years, and she remembers it fondly. Her childhood experiences of the home, including her memories of its open and airy expanses and the friendship her family developed with Scharoun, were formative for her.

Though Mrs. Zumpfe now lives in the Ruhr region of Germany, she still has a strong connection to the house. It was Julia Bojaryn of the Stiftung Haus Schminke, the foundation charged with conserving and protecting the house as a museum,[13] who put us in contact. Besides access during regular opening hours, audio guides, and tours, the museum also offers a special way of experiencing the house by allowing overnight stays by one party. This enabled us to spend time in the Schminke House after the other visitors and staff had retired for the evening, to enjoy it for ourselves and to observe more intensely the spaces Mrs. Zumpfe discussed during our conversation.

Born in 1930, Helga was the youngest of Charlotte and Fritz Schminke's four children (fig. 9). (The others were Erika, born in 1929; Traudel, or Gertraude, born in 1926; and Harald, born in 1924.) During our conversation, Mrs. Zumpfe lightheartedly took credit for the house coming into existence in the first place—as she claims, the Schminke's former residence became too small upon her arrival.

Although the family lived in the Modernist house from 1933 until 1951, all six Schminkes enjoyed it together for only one year: in 1934, Harald moved to Dresden to complete his high school diploma; he was enlisted in 1939 and died on the Russian front in 1943. Helga's father was largely absent after 1938 because of his involvement in the Sudeten crisis and World War II, during which he fought as a reconnaissance pilot and made only occasional visits home. Immediately after the war, from 1945 until 1948, he was held in captivity by the Russians.[14] However, the family also grew during the war by taking in Ello Hirschfeld, a daughter of Berlin friends of Scharoun's and Oskar Schlemmer's;[15] the girl, who had one Jewish grandparent, lived in the house for six years. Moreover, the Schminkes hosted family and friends, including Scharoun and his wife, Aenne, for many longer- and shorter-term visits (figs. 10, 11).

Scharoun became a close friend of the Schminke family through the house's design and construction and would spend time in Löbau over the years. Unable to pronounce "Professor Scharoun" as a young child, Helga called him "Pfeffer Huhuhun," and the nickname stuck. Mrs. Zumpfe recalls the excitement in the house when "Pfeffer" (pepper in English) was coming to visit and, in her words, "the big friendship" that developed. The relationship between Scharoun and the family continued even once they left Löbau, with Mrs. Zumpfe visiting him in Berlin after the war and later working with her parish to hire him to design a church and community space in Bochum.[16]

◀ Helga Zumpfe (née Schminke) photographed in her apartment in Bochum, 2015. **[8]**

The Schminke House is situated at Kirschallee 1B on a plot of land north of the family's pasta factory complex, Anker-Teigwaren, which Fritz inherited when he was 21 years old. In the 1930s, the small street led only to fields and farms, where the family got their milk. Decades after World War II, several other houses were constructed here, and in Mrs. Zumpfe's view "they don't fit." Indeed, the traditional pitched-roof dwellings contrast sharply with the Modernist form of the Schminke House.

Outdoor spaces form an integral part of the experience of the house, and for Mrs. Zumpfe they were the site of many memories (fig. 12). She remembers the children had free rein over the land: "We had the entire garden for play and at our disposal," she recalled. The only exception was in wintertime, when the Schminke parents demanded that the children leave the "snow landscape" intact, and in particular the space between the house and the circular large pond bootprint-free. The children

▼ Charlotte and Fritz Schminke and their four children: Harald (b. 1924), Helga (b. 1930), Erika (b. 1929), and Gertraude "Traudel" (b. 1926), from left to right. [9]

▲ Hans Scharoun at the table in the winter garden with Helga while visiting her family. [10]
▼ Scharoun reading to the children on the living room sofa. [11]

▲ The lush vegetation of the garden. **[12]**

took the longer path to the west and to the south to get to the large pond, which was turned into a skating rink.

In the summertime, the pond was even more intensively used with swimming, splashing, and "boating" in large wooden and metal laundry basins (figs. 13–17, 65–68). Mrs. Zumpfe treasures a small folded booklet that Scharoun made for the children, which includes a rhyming poem written by the architect and is illustrated with photographs of him and the children playing together in the large pond (figs. 19, 20).

There was a small bridge with a Scharoun-designed white bench between the large pond and its smaller, more overgrown counterpart where the children often played (fig. 18), and where Mrs. Zumpfe recalls listening to stories told by Aenne Scharoun, especially the Brothers Grimm tale "Einäuglein, Zweiäuglein und Dreiäuglein"

▲ The children playing with Scharoun in the large pond, with their father, Fritz, and Scharoun's wife, Aenne, on the bank. Helga is holding Scharoun's hands. [13]
▼ Scharoun (far right) being sprayed with water. Helga is standing in the pond. [14]

(One-Eye, Two-Eyes, and Three-Eyes). Above the pond stood a straw-roofed garden house, which predated the construction of the main house but was later renovated by Scharoun and became a place for play for the children. "And of course, we climbed on the trees," Mrs. Zumpfe said.

Another zone dedicated specifically to the children was found on the southwest side of the house, past the cantilevering entrance canopy and by the factory wall. Here, under the sprawling chestnut tree, was a large square sandbox, a swing, and gymnastics equipment (figs. 22, 45). There was also a little undulating track built on a tan-colored brick base, an apparatus invented and designed by Scharoun with the children in mind (figs. 21, 46). Helga and her siblings would sit in wagons not much larger than a shoebox and roll down the miniature rollercoaster. Closer to the house itself, adjoining the glazed zone of the winter garden to the south and the north, are brick-paved patios—extensions of the house used as additional areas for informal play (figs. 23, 47, 48).

◀ The children testing different tubs to use as boats in the large pond. **[15–17]**
▲ The children on the Scharoun-designed white bench between the two garden ponds. **[18]**

▲ An accordion-fold booklet that Scharoun made for the children, which Mrs. Zumpfe keeps as a memento. It includes a rhyming poem written by the architect and is illustrated with photographs of him and the children playing together in the large pond. **[19]**

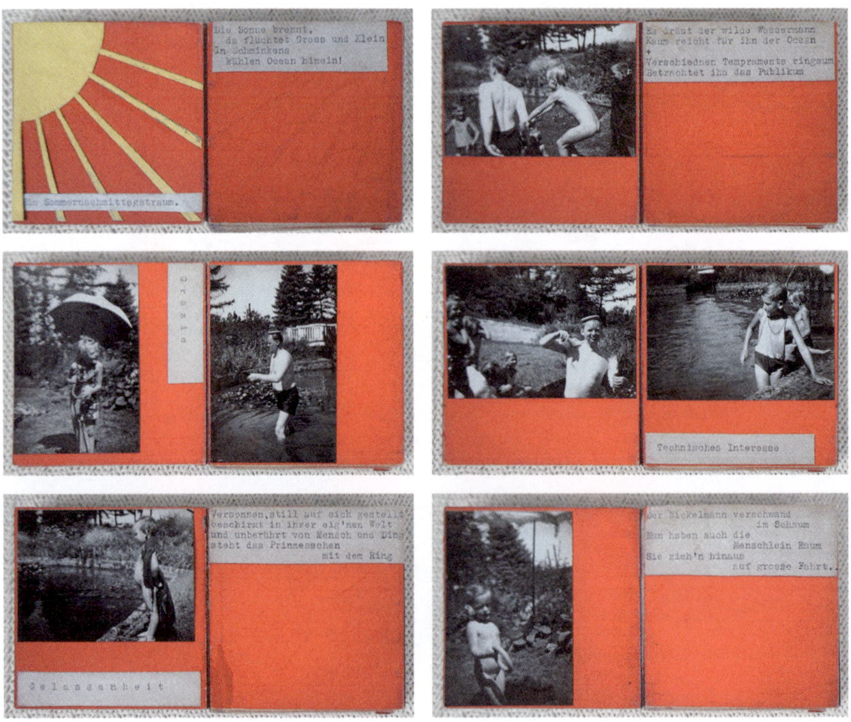

◄▲▼ Spreads from the booklet, which is signed by Scharoun, Aenne Scharoun and Alice Kerling, the photographer who documented the house in 1933. [20]

Inside the dwelling, the children moved about freely, and not only between the playroom and their bedrooms; they truly partook in and even shaped the life of the entire house. "The house was generous, and also for us children, always open and accessible," Mrs. Zumpfe recalled. The lower level, with its particularly spacious living quarters, was a place where she remembers spending a lot of time. Indeed, it is the open, bright, and expansive areas of the house that had the most lasting impression on our interlocutor: "My memories of the house are of the light— expanse and joy," she said, smiling (figs. 71, 72). "Overall, it is the spaciousness that we lived in in the house, but also equally in the garden—that is the most special memory."

◀ Helga standing at the gate between the pasta factory and the house, with the miniature rollercoaster and sandbox in the background. **[21]**
◀ The children playing in the sandbox, with the brick base of the rollercoaster in the foreground. **[22]**
▲ A view through the large porthole window from the playroom to the patio. **[23]**

The first space accessed from the main entrance is a double-height hall, a pivotal space in the house, where the living and service spaces cross and the diagonal stair ascends to the bedroom level above (figs. 24, 53). The hall spills into the children's playroom to the south and the dining room to the north, with both spaces joining fluidly and contributing to the house's emblematic openness. The dramatic angle of the stair was less significant to Helga as an organizational mechanism, however, than as a means to provide a long balustrade to slide down for fun (fig. 52).

▲ A view of the entry hall staircase and balustrade, with the large porthole window in the playroom visible to the right and living spaces beyond to the left. **[24]**
▶ The children's playroom, with Helga in the foreground. **[25]**
▶ The chalkboard and different storage spaces in the playroom, including the colored cubbies for each child on the western wall. **[26]**
▶ A view of the east wall of the playroom, including a photomontage by Scharoun of German ships and airplanes, a world map, nautical flags, and a swastika (the last of these added by Fritz Schminke, according to historian Klaus Kürvers). The table was added to the playroom later so the children could do their homework there. **[27]**

The children's playroom is at the core of the house, immediately to the right of the main entrance, and is one of the first spaces encountered by a visitor (figs. 5, 25–27, 49). The central placement of this room elevated the position of the children within the hierarchy of the home, giving them prominence and celebrating their presence.[17] "We played very intensely there!" Mrs. Zumpfe said. Several specific moments in the playroom stand out in her mind: a large chalkboard on the west

wall was used for drawings and later for homework (fig. 51).[18] And each child had a cubby in the adjacent built-in shelves and storage; stacked vertically, the cube spaces had doors that were each painted a different color. "Mine was yellow," Mrs. Zumpfe recalled, and—appropriately for the youngest child—"it was at the very bottom."

In the playroom, running along the large window subdivided by a grid of mullions, is a wide windowsill low enough that it could be used by the children for play. Historical photographs show Helga and Erika sitting on the ledge on small Thonet

▼ Helga (left) and Erika playing on the windowsill on their small Thonet chairs. **[28, 29]**

▲ Helga standing beside one of the doors with colored glass portholes. [30]

chairs (figs. 28, 29). The sill also allows access to two square, operable windows through which the children would clamber outside (fig. 50). This placement of the windows was not coincidental, as similar windows in the living room and winter garden are positioned much higher. Rather, the architect intentionally created opportunities for the children to manipulate and influence their surroundings, literally linking the inside and outside world for them.

Another special instance of Scharoun's child-focused design are the pairs of colored pieces of glass set into the metal frames of the exterior doors at a child's eye level (figs. 30, 76–80). These "colored portholes" were placed strategically so that "one could look through as a child and always see the world in a different color," Mrs. Zumpfe said. "And that was always special! I always went from one window to the other to see the world in different colors." The doors were a magical experience for the children, turning their view orange, amber, red, or blue.

▲ The children reading together on the living room sofa. [31]

The transparency and openness of the house's living spaces and the seamless transitions between them made hide-and-seek a challenge. Anyone hiding behind the long living room sofa, for example, would be found very quickly. "It was hard to find a place to hide," Mrs. Zumpfe said. "You should try it!" she added, laughing. She recalls teasing by and quarrels with her siblings, and being the youngest, she sometimes wished she had more places to escape to. She shared one story of an attempt to run away after squabbles with her brother and sisters; she made it only as far as the winter garden or the pond, to her own sorrow and the joy of her siblings. Along those lines, when asked what she would have changed or added to the house, she answered jokingly: "Mouseholes." The only time that she truly did not appreciate the openness of the dwelling was during thunderstorms, when her fear made her feel that it was perhaps too open.

Scharoun's design does incorporate curtains to create more intimate conditions in the living spaces if desired. The curtains along the facade would be closed in the living room on winter evenings, when board games or music were played and the family read out loud by the fireplace (figs. 4, 31, 70, 71). A thick interior curtain could also separate the playroom from the rest of the double-height entry hall. In Mrs. Zumpfe's memories, however, this curtain was usually drawn back, so that the children could "play everywhere."

▲ The winter garden seen from the threshold of the living room. **[32]**
▼ Erika and Helga (left) among the plants in the winter garden. **[33]**

▲ Views of the girls' bedroom with both beds unfolded (left) and with one bed stowed away and the desk folded out (right). [34, 35]

The service spaces of the house don't feature prominently in Mrs. Zumpfe's recollections, though she did remark that the children were obliged to help diligently in the Frankfurter Küche-influenced kitchen, with its characteristic wall-mounted, labeled aluminum dry-goods storage.[19] She recalls being afraid to go down to the basement of the home, a fear many children might empathize with. Besides the typical utilitarian functions, the basement accommodated a darkroom, where Charlotte Schminke developed the many photographs she took of family life. "She photographed a lot," Mrs. Zumpfe said, and her photos, as well as some film footage, offer a rich source of information about the way the home was used.

Visiting the house as an adult, Mrs. Zumpfe particularly appreciates the winter garden: "it was very special!" she emphasized (figs. 32, 72–75). Here, the family often took their meals and had Easter breakfast at a festively set table. It was also where the Christmas tree stood before the war; it was later placed in the hall because of blackouts. In the winter garden, beside the round table and its Mies van der Rohe-designed red-painted metal-tube chairs, was a birdcage with many small birds.[20] Charlotte's photographs show the girls playing in the sunken zone of the garden, among the plants (fig. 33).

Upstairs, the bedrooms of the children are very small, especially by today's standards, and in their layout are reminiscent of the sleeping cabins of a ship. Scharoun included a wall of built-in wardrobes in the generous hallway outside the bedrooms, so the rooms functioned primarily as places to sleep (fig. 55). Each of the two children's rooms originally had a pair of beds that folded up against the wall, like in a cabin of a ship (figs. 34, 35, 58). One of the rooms was later transformed into a bedroom for Harald, the oldest and the only boy, and as a result, the girls'

▼ The children on the upper terrace, looking out toward the garden. **[36]**

▲ The family outside of the house; Helga is playing with her mother, Charlotte. [37]

bedroom gained a space subtracted from Harald's room as an additional sleeping nook (fig. 59). "It was a very small space, where we slept," Mrs. Zumpfe confirmed. In fact, during the war, while her father was away, she slept in his bed in the parents' bedroom "so that the others could have more space" (figs. 60, 61). It was in her parents' room that Helga found a pair of scissors her mother had packed in a suitcase for an upcoming trip—which the girl used to crop her own hair, making her easily recognizable in photos from that period (fig. 36).

Childhood friends who came to visit the house liked it very much and were "always happy to be there." Yet what may have seemed natural to children wasn't always so to adults. In the small town of Löbau, there was sometimes talk of the "rich Schminkes" and their "strange home," Mrs. Zumpfe remembered. People walking down the Kirschallee "always looked inside" to the very open interiors, as the curtains were rarely closed. The neighbors gave the house the nickname "Nudeldampfer" (Noodle Steamer), alluding to the pasta factory and the ship-like form and nautical references of the architecture.

At the time, living in the extraordinary house was "normal" to Mrs. Zumpfe, while now she is more discerning and attuned to its idiosyncrasies, as well as its overall spaciousness and generosity. She is conscious that she sees the house differently now as an adult than she saw it as a child. "Als Kind lebt man und erlebt man nicht!"—as a child one "lives" and does not "experience consciously"—she pointed out emphatically. This distinction is vital in her appreciation of the matter-of-factness with which children approach and adapt to their circumstances. "I think that for children everything is normal," she said. Mrs. Zumpfe became a dedicated educator in a Waldorf kindergarten, and these statements are a reflection of her broader education and experiences. They are also, inevitably, a demonstration of her personal attitudes and predispositions. Although the upbringing that the Schminke children had was privileged in many ways, her recollections of the past are not prideful or boastful; instead, they are remarkably down-to-earth. A gentle humbleness colors her descriptions of the home. As a child she was not aware of the building's architectural significance or its avant-garde characteristics—this awareness came only much later, once she had moved. "It was simply where we lived," she said.

Living in the house was a very uplifting experience for Mrs. Zumpfe, and the freedoms it allowed have directly affected her thinking and her choices over the years. She has an artistic predisposition and has always been interested in creative activity, including puppeteering, storytelling and writing.[21] She believes that "the house, and through it Scharoun, has been very influential" in her upbringing and her interests. "I do think that the environment where people live changes them," she affirmed.

In 1948, Mrs. Zumpfe left the house for Dresden, where she pursued a stonemasonry apprenticeship rebuilding the Zwinger palace, which was destroyed during the war. She married and had two children of her own. After moving frequently over the course of her life, living in cramped dwellings, sometimes without basic amenities, she eventually settled in Bochum. She has lived in the same apartment for several decades now and appreciates certain of its qualities and the view that it

offers (figs. 38, 39). Besides stripping away many of the deteriorated finishes, one of the first things she did after moving in was to replace all of the interior doors with curtains, as in the ground floor of the Schminke House, to make the spaces more interconnected. The view out to nature, the ample daylight, and the flow of spaces one into another are for Mrs. Zumpfe references to the aspects of her childhood home that she remembers so happily. Her small-scale interventions may only approximate the spatial principles behind the Schminke House, but they are also a true testament to the lasting impression that its version of Modernist domesticity had on her. "I still dream about the house in Löbau. In the dreams, I walk around the house and events take place there," she said, smiling.

▲ Mrs. Zumpfe's apartment in Bochum, where she removed all the interior doors and replaced them with curtains, as in the living room of her childhood home. Photos of the Schminke House are prominently displayed on the walls of Mrs. Zumpfe's apartment. **[38, 39]**

▶ Stills from Helga Zumpfe's conversation with the authors, 2015. **[40]**

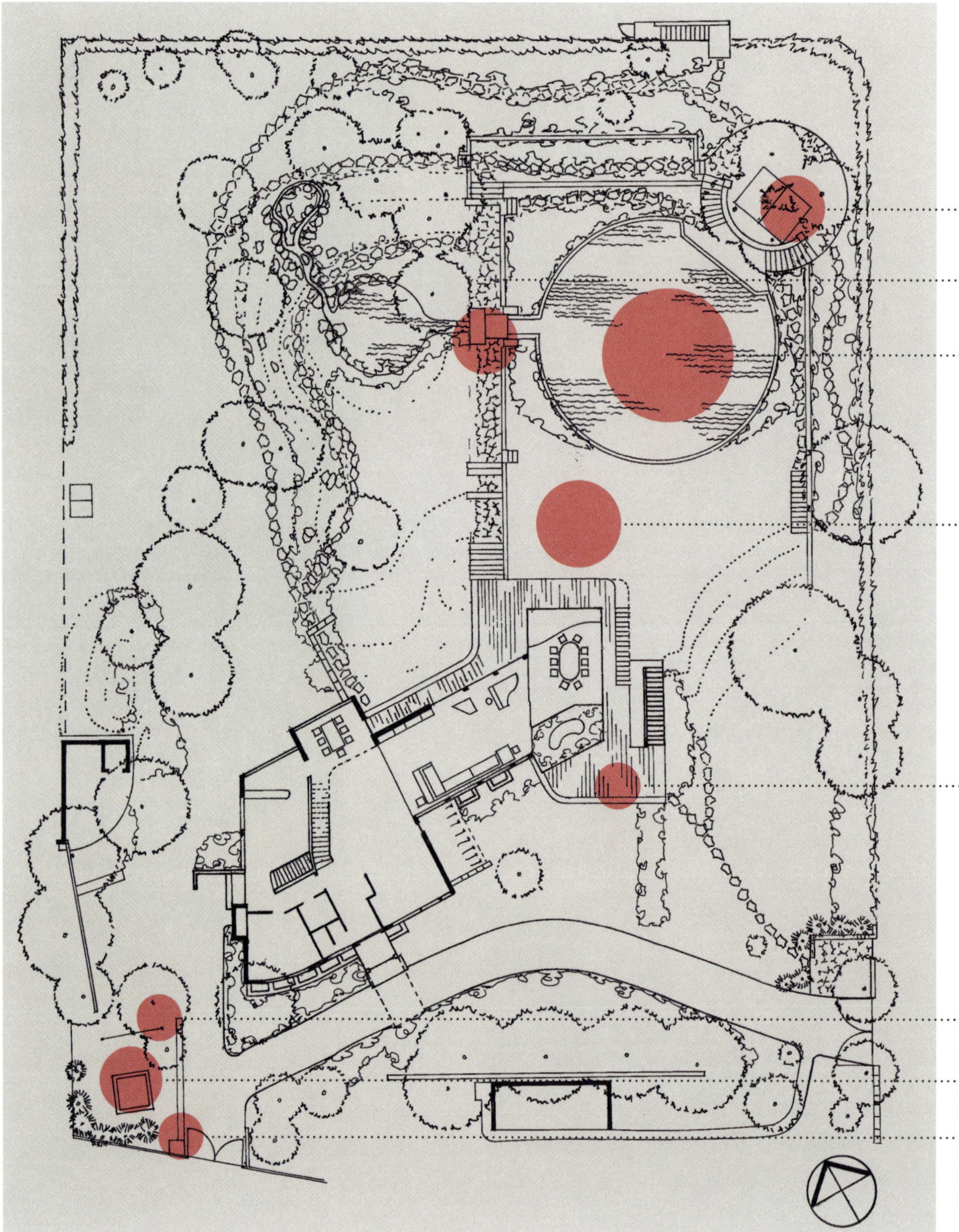

◀ A site plan with annotations referencing Mrs. Zumpfe's memories. **[41]**

Straw-roofed garden house, which predated the construction of the main house but was later renovated by Scharoun and became a place for play for the children

White bench between the two ponds, where Aenne Scharoun, the wife of Hans Scharoun, told stories to the children (fig. 18)

Large pond where the children played and swam in the summer and skated in the winter (figs. 12–17, 65–68)

Area between the house and the large pond; one of the few rules the children had to follow when playing outside was to leave the area free of bootprints in the winter

Brick-paved patio that was a zone of informal play (figs. 23, 47, 48)

Large chestnut tree, which Mrs. Zumpfe remembered as a canopy for the play space by the gate to her father's pasta factory

Swing, gymnastics equipment, and sandbox (figs. 22, 45)

Undulating track on a tan-colored brick base, designed by Scharoun; the children would sit in small wagons with wheels and roll down the miniature rollercoaster (figs. 21, 46)

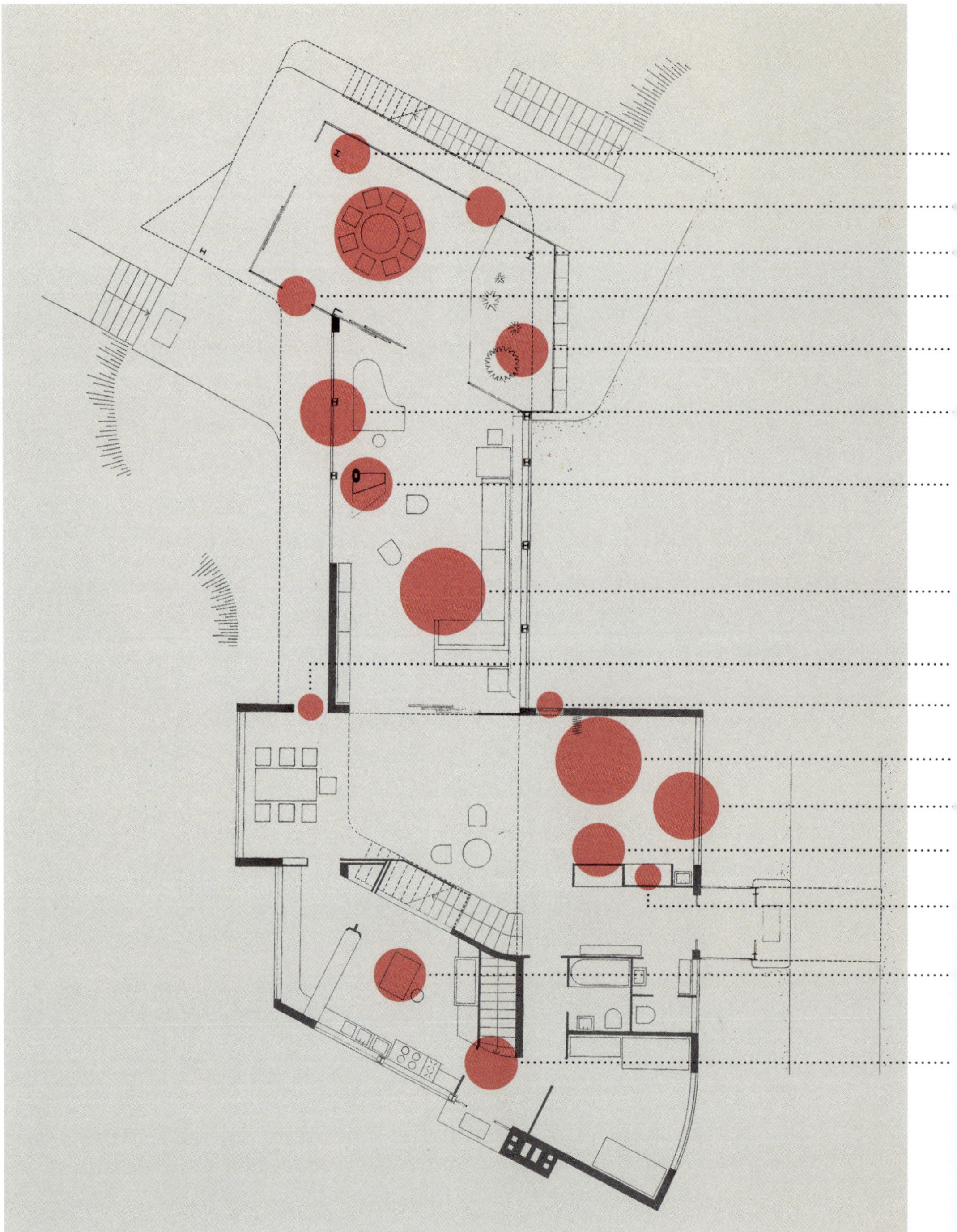

◀ A main-level plan with annotations referencing Mrs. Zumpfe's memories. **[42]**

Location of a large birdcage with many small birds, kept in the winter garden

Door with amber-colored glass portholes, at a child's eyelevel; Mrs. Zumpfe remembered running from door to door to see the world in different colors (figs. 75–77)

Winter garden table: a place for meals and for festive celebrations (figs. 10, 72, 73)

Door with blue-colored glass portholes (figs. 30, 78)

Sunken indoor garden full of lush plants (figs. 32, 33, 74)

Curtains along the facade would be closed on winter evenings and during thunderstorms, the only time when the house felt too open to Helga (fig. 71)

Freestanding fireplace, removed after the family left the house (figs. 4, 71)

Living room sofa, where board games or music were played and the family read out loud in the evenings (figs. 11, 31)

Door with orange-colored glass portholes (fig. 80)

Large circular window toward patio (figs. 23, 24, 48)

Children's playroom (figs. 5, 49)

Wide windowsill and two square, operable windows, through which the children would go outside (figs. 28, 29, 50)

Large chalkboard used for drawings and later for homework (figs. 26, 51)

Individual storage cubbies for each of the children with doors each painted a different color; Helga's was yellow and was at the bottom of the stack (figs. 26, 51)

Kitchen, where the children were obliged to help diligently

Stairs to the basement. The underground space frightened Helga. Beside service spaces it contained Charlotte Schminke's darkroom

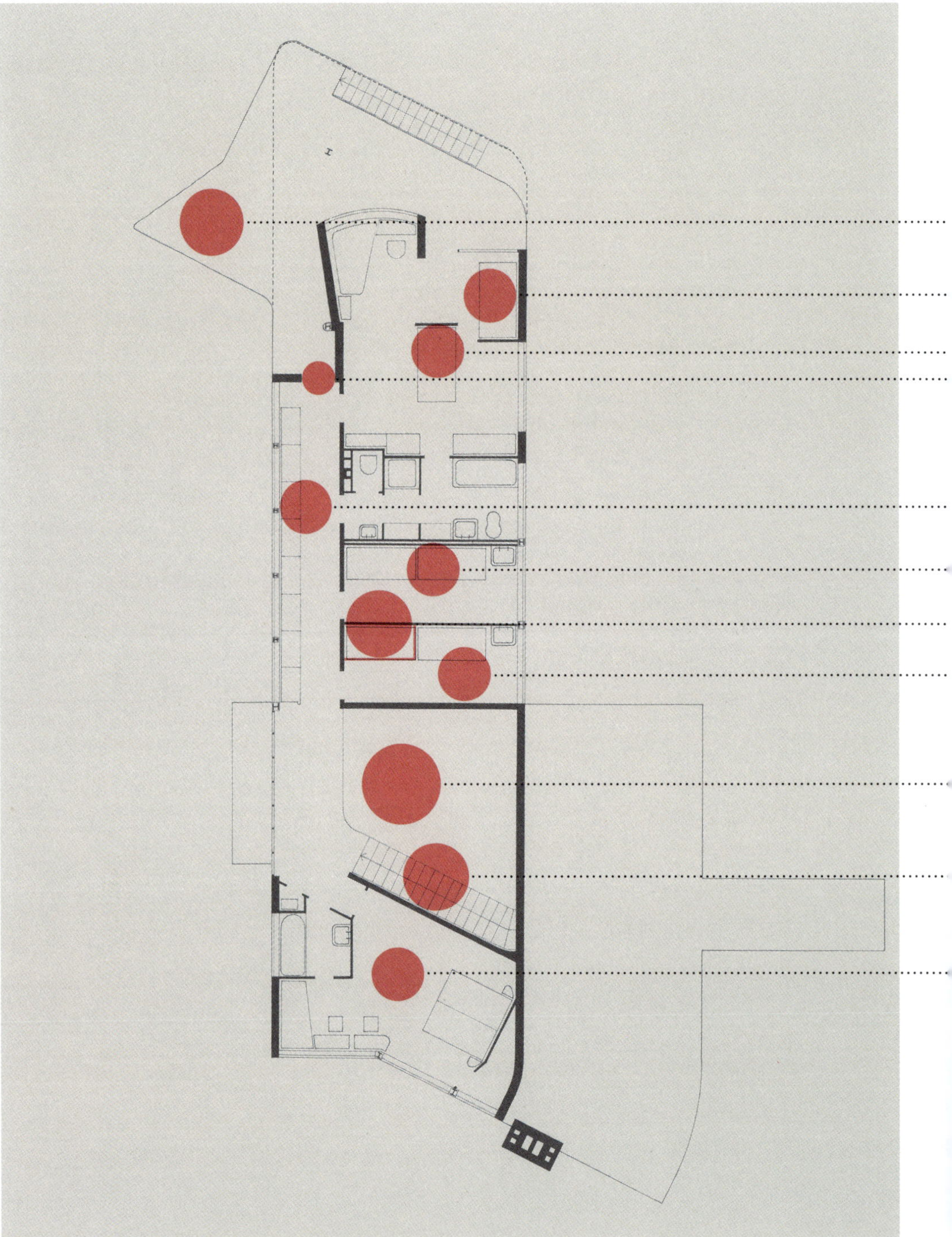

◀ An upper-level plan with annotations referencing Mrs. Zumpfe's memories. **[43]**

Cantilevering upper terrace with a view of the garden (figs. 36, 62, 63)

Helga's mother's bed (figs. 60, 61)

Helga's father's bed, where Helga slept when he was away during the war (figs. 60, 61)

Door with red-colored glass portholes (fig. 79)

Wall of storage in the hallway, where the children kept their clothes, leaving their rooms as just places to sleep (fig. 55)

Folding beds of the girls' bedroom (figs. 34, 35, 58)

Sleeping nook, subtracted from Harald's room, giving the girls' room three beds (fig. 59)

Bedroom of Harald, the oldest and only boy of the four siblings

Double-height space of the entry hall; the spaciousness of the house is one of the most enduring memories for Mrs. Zumpfe (figs. 5, 24, 53)

Balustrade of the stair, which the children slid on (fig. 52)

Guest suite, where Scharoun would stay when visiting the family (figs. 56, 57)

◄◄ The entrance of the Schminke House, where Helga Zumpfe lived from 1933 to 1948, photographed in 2015. **[44]**

◄ A view from the entrance canopy looking to the children's play area under the chestnut tree. Originally there was a large sandbox, a swing, and gymnastics equipment here. The wall to the left separated the house from the family's pasta factory next door. **[45]**

▲ The little undulating track built on a tan-colored brick base (in foreground) was designed by Scharoun specifically with the children in mind. They would sit in small wagons not much larger than a shoebox with wheels on the track and roll down the miniature rollercoaster. Historical photos show that the track was once significantly more elevated off the ground (see figs. 21, 22). **[46]**

▲ A tiled patio outside the winter garden, where the children played. **[47]**
► The large porthole window in the children's playroom, looking onto the patio. **[48]**

►► Each child had an individual cubby in the playroom. Helga's was yellow and at the bottom of the stack, as she was the youngest. **[49]**

▲ The wide windowsill in the playroom was low enough for the children to play on. The adjacent window has two operable sashes, through which the children would clamber outside. These openings appear in the bottom row in only the playroom window; they were specified higher elsewhere in the house. **[50]**

▶ The chalkboard in the playroom, which was used by the children for drawing and later for homework. **[51]**

▼ The children would slide down the staircase's long balustrade. Under the stair is the entrance to the pantry and kitchen. [52]

▶ The dining room is framed by the ascending stair and faces the playroom off the generous entry hall. [53]

▲ The windows at the top of the staircase, overlooking the garden. [54]
► A wall of built-in wardrobes was provided in the hallway outside the bedrooms, so the rooms themselves functioned primarily as places to sleep. [55]

◄ The guest bathroom, with doors leading directly to the hallway and to the guest room itself. [56]
▲ The guest bedroom, where Scharoun stayed when he visited Löbau. The architect and the family developed a friendship during the planning and construction of the house, and maintained a close relationship even after World War II and into Mrs. Zumpfe's adulthood. [57]

▲ The girls' bedroom, which was originally fitted with a sink and had beds and a desk that folded up against the wall. **[58]**

▶ A nook was later subtracted from Harald's room and annexed into the girls' room to give them additional sleeping space. **[59]**

▲ There was originally a wall at the head of Helga's father's bed in the center of the parents' bedroom. **[60]**

► During the war, while her father was away, Helga slept in his bed in her parents' bedroom. **[61]**

◄◄ The terrace off Helga's parents' bedroom, which projects into and provides a view of the garden. **[62]**

◄▲ A stair leading from the parents' terrace directly to the patio below and into the garden. **[63, 64]**

▼ A view of the large pond with neighboring houses in the background. These were built along the Kirschallee decades after World War II, and Mrs. Zumpfe contends that they "don't fit." **[65]**
▶ The area around the pond was one of the children's favorite play spaces. In the winter, however, they were forbidden from walking in the space between the house and pond, so their parents could enjoy the view of the unmarked snow. **[66]**

◀ The house was nicknamed the "Nudeldampfer" (Noodle Steamer) by the people of Löbau, in reference to Fritz Schminke's pasta factory next door and the allusions to nautical elements in Scharoun's design. **[67]**

▲ The children swam in the pond in the summer and ice-skated on it in the winter. **[68]**

◄ Stone steps approaching the house from the garden. **[69]**
▲ A freestanding fireplace near the picture window originally defined a zone for the piano within the living room. **[70]**

◄◄ The openness of the house is one of Mrs. Zumpfe's strongest memories, exemplified here in the transition from the living room to the garden and the winter garden. [71]

▲ The family often took their meals and celebrated holidays in the winter garden before the war; this is where the Christmas tree stood and where Easter breakfast was served. [72]
► Beside the table stood a large birdcage, home to many small birds. [73]

▼ Reflecting on the house now, Mrs. Zumpfe finds the winter garden to be the most special place in the home. **[74]**

▶ The circular motif of the ceiling and the portholes in the doors leading out to the garden. **[75]**

▶▶ Scharoun intentionally placed these portholes at the children's eye level. Mrs. Zumpfe recalls running from door to door to look at the world through different-color glass. **[76]**

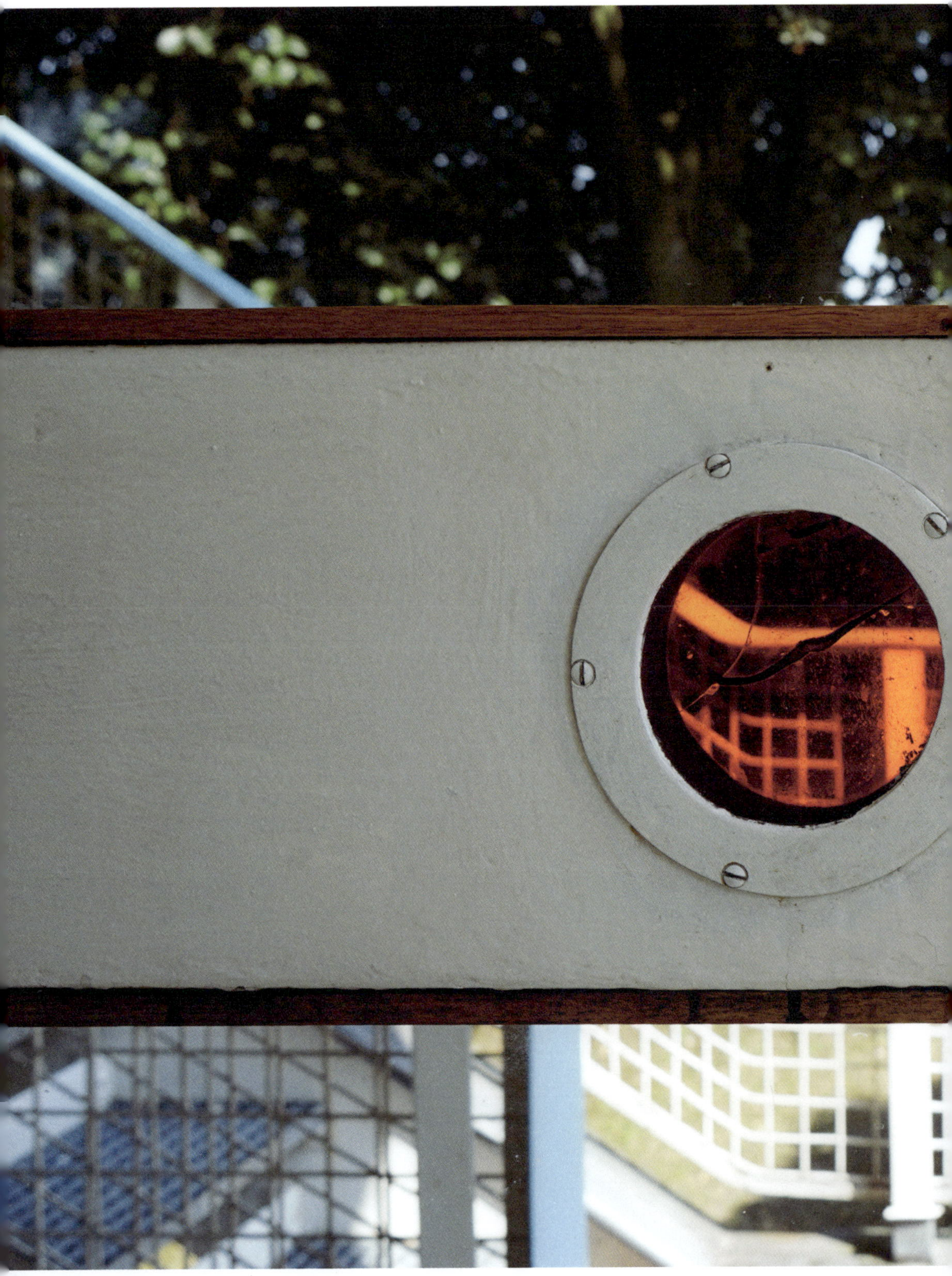

◀ A view through the amber glass in the east door of the winter garden. **[77]**

◀ A blue view through the west door of the winter garden. **[78]**

◀ A red view through a door in the upstairs corridor. **[79]**

▲ An orange view through the dining room door. **[80]**

▶▶ The house illuminated in the evening. **[81]**

Notes

1 Peter Blundell Jones, "A Forty Year Encounter with Hans Scharoun: Commentary on the Submission of a PhD by Publication" (supplement to dissertation, the University of Sheffield, June 2013), 43, https://core.ac.uk/download/pdf/20344024.pdf; Carsten Krohn, *Hans Scharoun: Buildings and Projects*, trans. Julian Reisenberger (Basel: Birkhäuser, 2018), 68. Blundell Jones calls the house "unrestrainedly modernist" and Krohn labels it a "pioneering work of organic architecture."

2 "The Schminke House was the last house designed by Scharoun in an overtly Modernist way before the Nazis imposed a compulsory vernacular style, after which Scharoun was obliged to disguise his houses externally while continuing his experiments within." Flora Samuel and Peter Blundell Jones, "The Making of Architectural Promenade: Villa Savoye and Schminke House," *arq: Architectural Research Quarterly* 16, no. 2 (June 2012): 108–24.

3 For documentation of the cultural milieu of Breslau at the time, including progressive attitudes toward the use of color (among other aspects of architecture), see Deborah Ascher Barnstone, *Beyond the Bauhaus: Cultural Modernity in Breslau, 1918–33* (Ann Arbor: University of Michigan Press, 2016).

4 Krohn, *Hans Scharoun*, 8.

5 J. Christoph Bürkle, *Hans Scharoun*, trans. Pamela Johnson (Zurich: Artemis, 1993), 84.

6 Peter Blundell Jones, *Hans Scharoun* (London: Phaidon Press, 1995), 77.

7 Krohn, *Hans Scharoun*, 11. The term "inside outwards" was used by Theodor Fischer and later Hugo Häring, as Peter Blundell Jones points out in *Hugo Häring: The Organic versus the Geometric* (Stuttgart: Edition Axel Menges, 1999).

8 The stepped landscape was initially prepared for an English-style country home that Fritz Schminke's father never had the chance to realize.

9 Peter Blundell Jones attributes the garden design to Herta Hammerbacher and Hermann Mattern in "Architect and Landscape Architect Working Together: Scharoun and Mattern," in *Relating Architecture to Landscape*, ed. Jan Birksted (London: E & FN Spon, 1999). Based in part on the dissertation of landscape architect Claudia Feltrup, Klaus Kürvers states, however, that there is no written or drawn evidence of Hammerbacher or Mattern designing the garden. Kürvers does note the influence of Hammerbacher in the planting of the garden and a record of Hammerbacher and Mattern visiting the Schminke House in 1933. For an in-depth study of the Schminke House, see Kürvers, "Entschlüsselung eines Bildes – Das Landhaus Schminke von Hans Scharoun" (dissertation, Berlin University of the Arts, 1996), http://klausk.berlin/architektur/publikationen/entschluesselung-eines-bildes/.

10 Samuel and Blundell Jones call it "a ship steaming across the garden." "Architectural Promenade," 122.

11 Samuel and Blundell Jones, "Architectural Promenade," 109.

12 Only one of Scharoun's projects, the apartment house in Siemensstadt, Berlin, is mentioned in Henry-Russell Hitchcock and Philip Johnson's *The International Style: Architecture since 1922* (New York: W. W. Norton, 1932), and not in

flattering terms: "The fenestration is arbitrary and complicated" (page 207). More generally, as Bürkle writes, "The selective way in which the history of Modernism has been written has meant that until recently it has been difficult to define the role of organic building in general, and the work of Hans Scharoun in particular, in 20th-century architecture." *Hans Scharoun*, 9.

13 "The Foundation," Stiftung Haus Schminke, accessed February 22, 2020, https://www.stiftung-hausschminke.eu/en/The-Foundation_2/54/#q54.

14 Fritz Schminke's involvement in World War II was recently investigated by his great granddaughter Anael Berkovitz; see Frank Seibel, "Ein ehrenwertes Haus," *Sächsische Zeitung*, October 18, 2017, https://www.saechsische.de/plus/ein-ehrenwertes-haus-3797827.html.

15 Ello's father had one Jewish parent and had to flee the Nazi regime, while her mother had severe multiple sclerosis and could not take care of the young girl.

16 After the war, Scharoun also produced a design for a house in Celle for Fritz Schminke, which was never realized.

17 Klaus Kürvers makes this point in the 2012 film *Built with Light: A Ship of Life from Hans Scharoun*, directed by Kerstin Stutterheim and Niels Bolbrinker.

18 Later, as the children grew older, a table was placed in the playroom so they could do their homework there as well.

19 In the case of the Schminke House, the storage fit neatly in the space below the stair. For a history of the Frankfurt Kitchen, see Juliet Kinchin and Aidan O'Connor, *Counter Space: Design and the Modern Kitchen* (New York: Museum of Modern Art, 2011). For information on its designer, Grete Schütte-Lihotzky, see Carmen Espegel, *Women Architects in the Modern Movement* (New York: Routledge, 2018).

20 The family also had pet rabbits, which lived in a stall outside, and Helga's mother kept chickens in a coop on the grounds of the house. There were a number of farm animals that belonged to the pasta factory, as well: chickens, turkeys, pigs, and others.

21 Helga Zumpfe authored the book *Aus dem Tagebuch der kleinen Kinder: Ein Blick in die Kleinkindzeichnungen* (From the Diary of Small Children: A Look at Children's Drawings) (Borchen, Germany: Ch. Möllmann, 2002).

Unité d'Habitation

Le Corbusier
Marseille, France
1952

The Unité d'Habitation was Le Corbusier's response to the dire need for housing in France after the destruction of World War II.[1] The first realization of the architect's approach to high-density housing, the building in Marseille was a laboratory of new construction techniques and material applications.[2] More significantly, however, it was also a culmination of the architect's research and a direct representation of his ideas about individual and collective living. "It was more than just housing, it was more even than just architecture: it proposed a way of life," Robert Furneaux Jordan claims.[3] As Jacques Sbriglio asserts, Le Corbusier was "building the framework of a changing society."[4]

The country's first Minister for Reconstruction, Raoul Dautry, awarded the commission for the Unité to Le Corbusier in 1945; the architect later wrote that he accepted the task on the condition that he would be "free of all building regulations in force."[5] Through the project, the architect and his team questioned conventions and redefined the standards and expectations for contemporary housing, from the urban scale (by favoring density in a park-like setting) to that of the individual room (integrating the kitchen in the living spaces) and even the smallest fixtures (ergonomic wooden door handles).[6] Based on his Modulor system of measure, the scheme responds to Le Corbusier's ideas of universal beauty through proportion, but also to the needs of different age groups who would occupy the apartments (fig. 4).[7]

Le Corbusier used the analogy of wine bottles in a rack to describe the relationship between the Unité apartments and the framework of the block. The building, which operated as social housing for the first three years after it opened,[8] accom-

▲ An aerial view of the Unité d'Habitation in Marseille. [1]

modates 337 families in 23 different unit variations. The prototypical unit types are "top-down" and "bottom-up" interlocking maisonettes. This skip-stop sectional organization results in corridor spaces—or "interior streets," as Le Corbusier termed them—that appear on only seven of the building's eighteen floors. This arrangement increases functional efficiency and provides multiple exposures for daylight and opportunities for cross ventilation in the majority of apartments. Le Corbusier aimed to provide access to nature within the units, on the communal roof, and through the permeable base of the building, which is raised on massive pilotis. The architecture further responds to the Mediterranean climate through its characteristic brise-soleils, the roughness of the concrete, and an intensity of applied color.

▲ Children with educator Lilette Ripert (Madame Ougier) on the rooftop of the Unité. [2]
▼ A section and plan of the rooftop of the Unité d'Habitation. Blanche Lemco van Ginkel worked on the design of the rooftop while at Le Corbusier's office. [3]

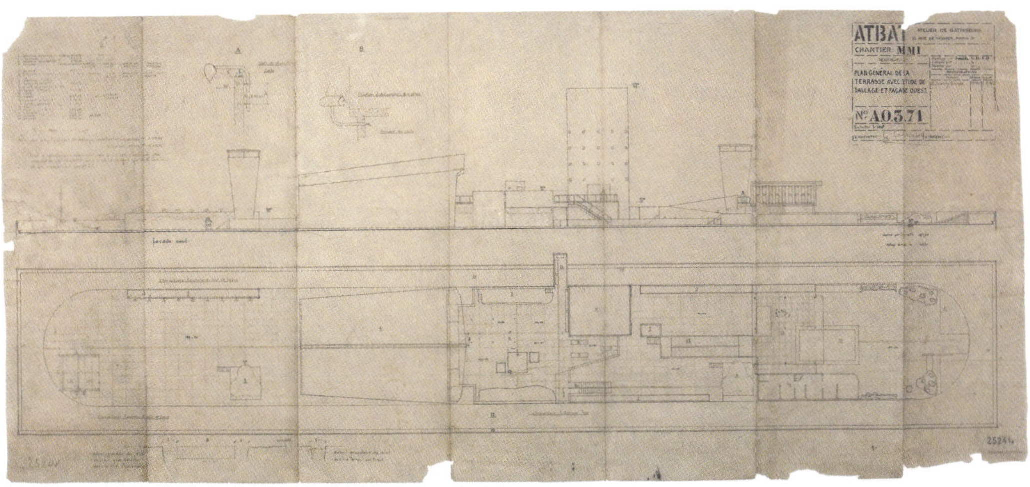

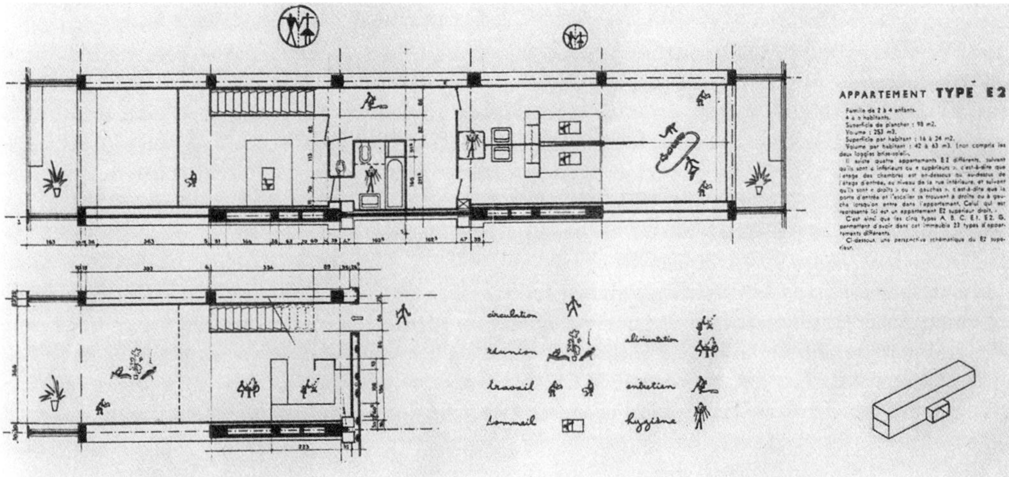
APPARTEMENT TYPE E2
circulation
réunion
travail
sommeil
alimentation
entretien
hygiène

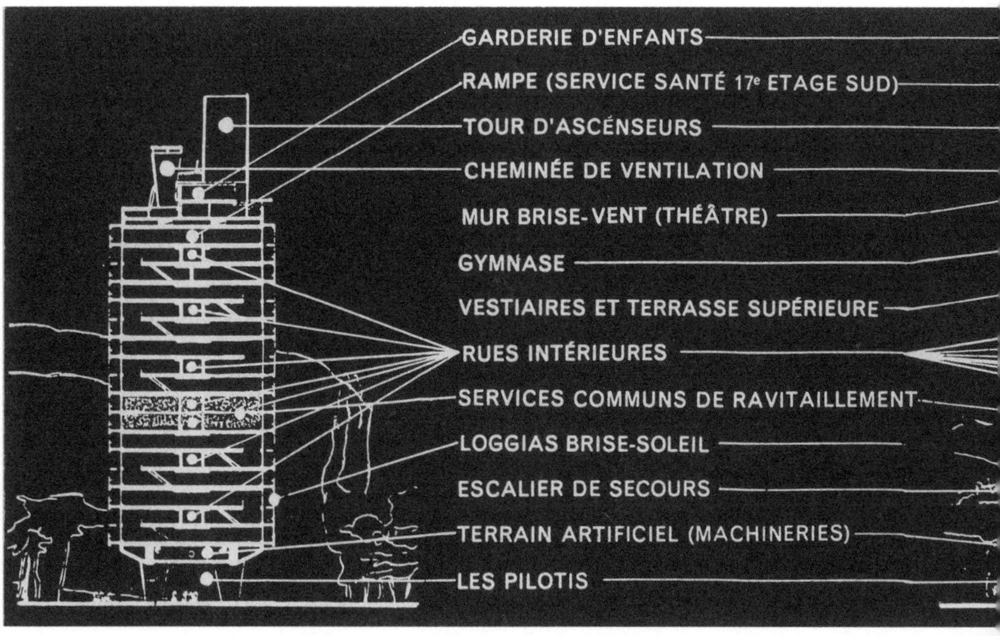
GARDERIE D'ENFANTS
RAMPE (SERVICE SANTÉ 17e ETAGE SUD)
TOUR D'ASCÉNSEURS
CHEMINÉE DE VENTILATION
MUR BRISE-VENT (THÉÂTRE)
GYMNASE
VESTIAIRES ET TERRASSE SUPÉRIEURE
RUES INTÉRIEURES
SERVICES COMMUNS DE RAVITAILLEMENT
LOGGIAS BRISE-SOLEIL
ESCALIER DE SECOURS
TERRAIN ARTIFICIEL (MACHINERIES)
LES PILOTIS

From the individual freedoms it aimed to allow to its collective amenities (figs. 2, 3, 5) the Unité has become a model for housing and continues to be studied, copied, and misappropriated.[9] In his book *Modern Housing Prototypes*, Roger Sherwood covers common criticisms of the building, noting its narrow apartments, dark hallways, and dysfunctional shopping street. "Still," he writes, "the Marseilles block is probably the most copied building of the twentieth century. Its influence on the form of subsequent housing has been profound, and variations of it can be seen in almost every country, built under widely varying conditions. It may be a monument disguised as housing, but modern housing and the Unité d'Habitation are synonymous."[10]

◀ An annotated drawing by Le Corbusier of the typical skip-stop Unité apartment type, with icons indicating spaces for adults and children as well as intended uses. **[4]**
▼ Short and long sections indicating all of the communal amenities of the building by Le Corbusier. **[5]**

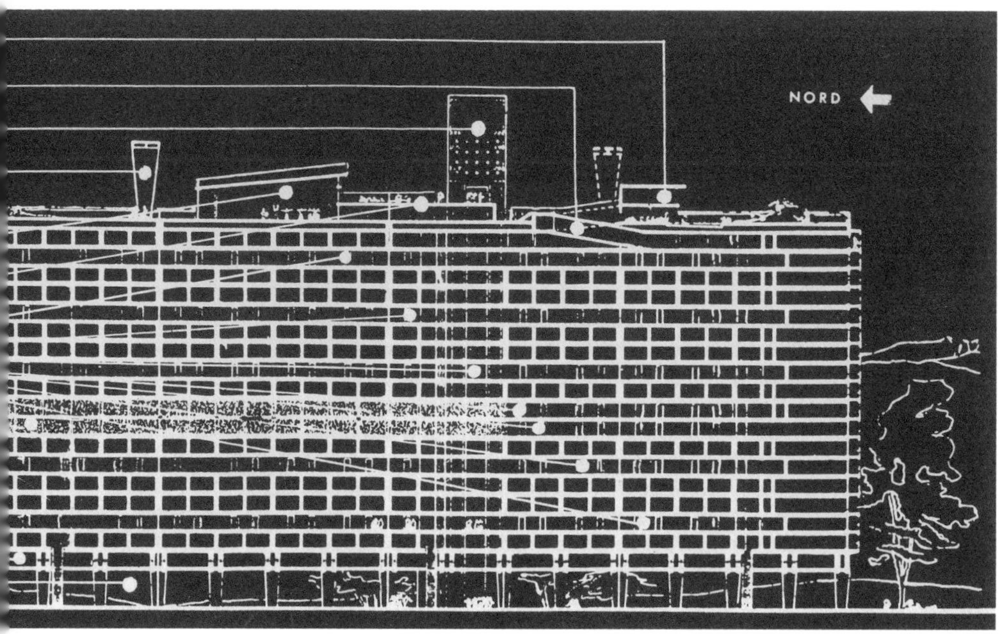

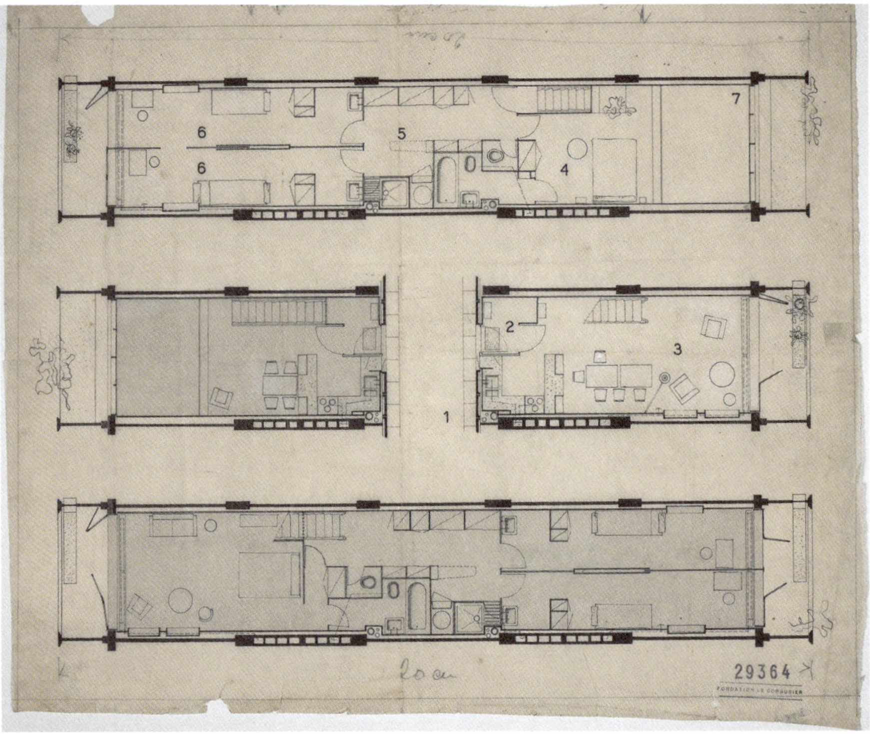

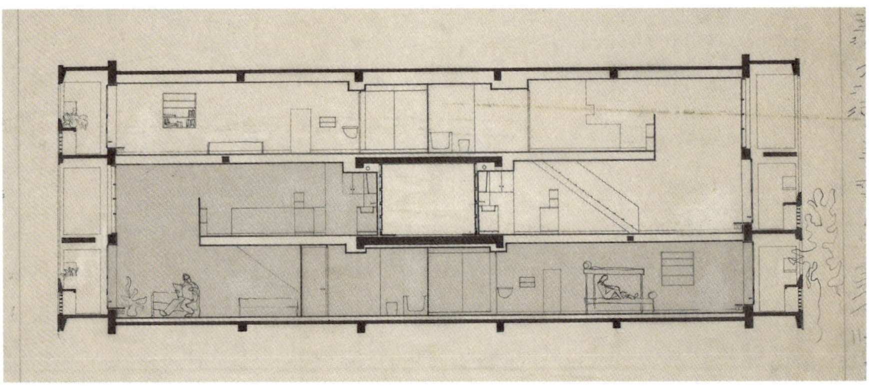

▲ Plans (top) and section (bottom) of two typical, interlocking skip-stop apartments by Le Corbusier. [6, 7]

► Gisèle Moreau photographed in her apartment in the Unité d'Habitation, 2015. [8]

Conversation with Gisèle Moreau

Gisèle Moreau moved into the newly completed Unité in 1953, when she was ten years old. Since then, she has experienced the apartment block from the perspectives of a child, a parent, and a grandparent. She is very enthusiastic about the building, its history, and the vision of Le Corbusier that it embodies: "I'm very proud of living here," she said. "It is enough to make me happy. I mean, who can say that they live in a historical[ly significant] building? … I never regretted living here, never."

She has lived in the Unité for most of her life, apart from periods studying in England and the United States and a brief time in a small house in Marseille, after her children were born. She moved back to "the Corbusier" when an apartment opened up across the hall from her childhood home and her mother urged her to return. "I came back with my husband in 1970 and I haven't moved since, and I probably won't move, ever," she said. The retired English teacher now lives in the unit where she grew up, which she inherited from her parents. In 2015, we conversed with Ms. Moreau in the upper-level sitting room of this apartment, having been introduced by Bénédicte Gandini from the Fondation Le Corbusier.

When it first opened, the building belonged to the city, so civil servants and employees of the state had priority in obtaining apartments. Ms. Moreau's father was in the French Air Force. Having served in French Indochina, he was relocated back to Marseille after World War II. "My mother fell in love with this [building] and my father was very much interested, so this is why they moved here," she recalled. When they moved in, they were a family of four: Gisèle; her brother, three years her junior; and their parents. Two additional boys were born shortly after.[11] The children's grandmother also came to stay for months at a time; during these visits, the 98-square-meter (1,050-square-foot) apartment, which Ms. Moreau now occupies on her own, housed seven people.[12]

The building was more than shelter—moving in meant becoming part of a new community. "I was immediately part of a group of children. I had lots of friends

▼ The Unité block photographed under construction, 1951. **[9]**

▶ A girl on a scooter by the concrete pilotis. **[10]**

▲ Children running on the rooftop of the building. [11]

living in the building," Ms. Moreau recalled. "My best friend moved the day before, it was a Tuesday, and for me it was a Wednesday, [and we moved in] just opposite the corridor, that we call a street. We were of the same age and I still see her regularly." The relationships are a significant result not only of the building's density, but also of the urban conditions it created, where shared amenities were humanistic and not just utilitarian. Le Corbusier aimed "to make individual lodgings perfect in a big ensemble," according to Ms. Moreau. "I think he did a good job of that."

In 1953, the neighborhood surrounding the apartment block was more of a pastoral landscape than the urban setting it is today (fig. 9). "There were four farms around. I used to go for milk in a little tin can every evening. Can you imagine? ... It's unbelievable!" she explained, laughing. Concrete pilotis lift the boat-like mass of the

▲ Children playing with miniature sailboats in the rooftop wading pool. [12]

Unité from the ground, allowing for circulation under the building (figs. 10, 43). The garden at the base of the structure, with its lush vegetation and standard playground apparatus, is part of the public realm; though it does not belong to the building, it is frequently used by inhabitants (fig. 41).

Ms. Moreau's favorite place in the Unité is the roof. "It's a miracle," she said. "I still get a shock when the elevator opens and I see the sky and the sea, and it's great! I spent part of my life there looking after my brothers, my two daughters, my four grandchildren. And I picnicked in the evening and I studied my lessons and we played" (figs. 11, 12, 16–21, 68–72). She still goes up to the roof often: "Especially on summer evenings, when it gets cooler and it's still a little hot in the apartment, we go up and meet for aperitifs or a picnic. And we have events, too—it can be movies or dancing or music."

▲ Community events in the rooftop gymnasium: midnight mass (left), a school performance (middle), and an audience of schoolchildren watching a puppet show (right). [13–15]

The largest enclosed space on the roof is *le gymnase* (the gymnasium), and for the first three years of the building's occupation it hosted a number of communal activities: theater, dances, masses, a youth club, parties, communions, weddings (figs. 13–15). "When the apartments were sold individually, that was for sale, too, and it was bought by somebody who turned it into a sport gymnasium. I remember my father's reaction. It was a catastrophe for him," Ms. Moreau recalled. Several years ago, sparking much controversy among the residents, the space became a contemporary art gallery run by the designer Ora-ïto (fig. 73). Ms. Moreau is in favor of the endeavor. "I think it can only add to what we have to have an art gallery, but some people disagree with the idea," she says.

Since 2013, parts of the roof are accessible in the late afternoon and evening only to residents, including the shallow wading pool, meant for small children, and the concrete seating area surrounding it. The restriction grants residents more privacy in response to the large numbers of external visitors to the building. In 2014, according to Ms. Moreau, the number of tourists reached 80,000: "It's an invasion!" she exclaimed. Nevertheless, she generously gives tours and gladly speaks about her experiences. "I enjoy doing so, if people are interested, of course—I don't want to force that on them. Recently I went to see a doctor that knew my daughters, and my daughters are like me, because she said: 'When you [all] talk about Le Corbusier, you are so enthusiastic!' And I said, 'It's a family business!'"

▲ Children splashing in the rooftop wading pool. [16]

She also shared a special memory that she strongly associates with the amorphous concrete "rocks" on the roof (figs. 17, 18, 71). "This was the place where I was sitting with a friend, it was in August 1965. We were sunbathing and we had a little transistor on with music and all of a sudden the music stopped and the person said, 'We are very sad to announce the death of the very famous architect Le Corbusier.'" She conveyed her shock with her facial expression more than with words; the impact of the announcement was clear. Her personal association with the architect persists: "When I hear 'Le Corbusier'"—she said, turning her head side to side and looking behind her back—"I always imagine that they are talking about me. Wherever I am in the world, 'Le Corbusier,' oh—that's me! He is so very important for people who live here."

▲ Children sunbathing on a tilted concrete plane on the building's rooftop. [17]
▼ Children climbing on the amorphous concrete rock (left) and under the tilted concrete plane (right) on the rooftop. [18, 19]

▲ Children scaling a tilted concrete plane on the rooftop. This is one of Ms. Moreau's favorite photographs of the building. [20]
▼ Kids balancing between the concrete screens on the rooftop and the nursery over the wading pool. [21]

▲ A view looking down at the threshold between the double-height living space and the balcony of a typical apartment. [22]

The characteristic skip-stop layout of the apartments of the Unité results in units that have a double exposure for light and cross ventilation. "I still think that it's unusual because what I like in it is the light coming from both sides, from the east and the west," Ms. Moreau explained. "The apartments are very narrow—some people don't like that, but I don't mind. I like the double height of the room downstairs, the fact that there is a staircase so it can be a little like a house … . It's not luxurious at all, you know, not at all, but you don't have to pretend that it is. But that is the way I am too, so I like it," she added, laughing.

The apartments were augmented by adjoining outdoor spaces, accessible through generous openings (fig. 22). In the case of Ms. Moreau's family's unit—which had one of the most typical layouts, with the living room below and bedrooms above—that meant a double-height loggia on the east facade and a single-height one on the west (figs. 44–48). "As there was very little traffic, my mother used to open the four windows in May and close them in October," Ms. Moreau recalled. In this sense, the loggia really became an extension of the living space, as Le Corbusier

▲ Views of the children's rooms looking toward the exterior loggia (top) and toward the interior of the apartment (bottom), showing the sliding chalkboard that separated the rooms. **[23, 24]**

intended. Though traffic has increased, Ms. Moreau still continues the practice, allowing for ample cross ventilation and visually claiming the loggia as part of the spatial experience of the apartment: "I really do what Le Corbusier said—the extension of the lodging. It doesn't mean I go and sit there, but I think it gives more space to the room ... . Can you hear the cicadas?"

In Ms. Moreau's childhood apartment, the kids' bedrooms were located on the upper level facing west.[13] That is where she remembers spending most of her time as a child (figs. 23, 24, 54–56). "I think I liked my bedroom," she said. "When the babies started being born, maybe a little less, because, well ... " Nevertheless, she distinctly remembers the sliding blackboard that separated the two narrow rooms: "I studied on the blackboard from junior high until university. I used it a lot. A lot!" Each of the children's rooms had its own washbasin, and they shared a shower (figs. 25, 57). At the time, these were incredible amenities for what was considered "cheap lodgings for poor people." "A bathroom for the parents a shower, and two washbasins for the children—that was exceptional! That's what my mother thought: wonderful!" Ms. Moreau affirmed.

▼ A child entering the shower cabin. **[25]**

▶ A woman dressing a baby on the built-in changing table in the parents' bedroom. **[26]**

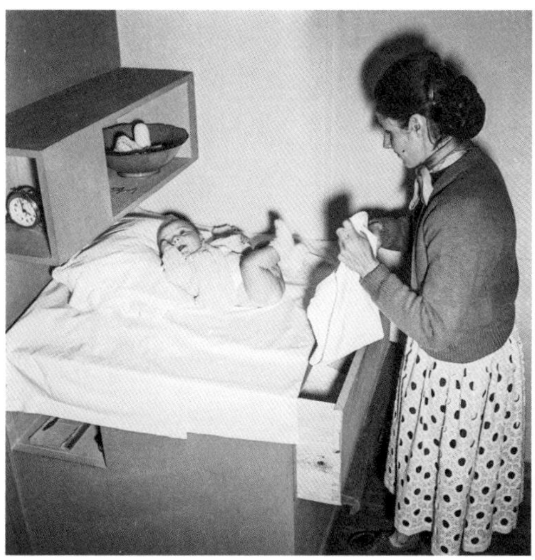

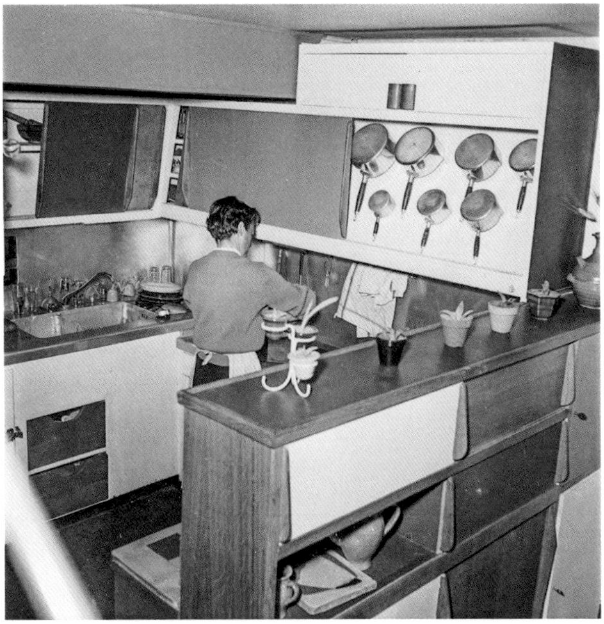

▲ Every Unité kitchen was identical, regardless of the apartment's size. [27]

The parents' bedroom was located on the mezzanine overlooking the living room, facing east (figs. 49, 53, 58). It was very open, which was not a welcome feature when a teenage Ms. Moreau began to go out by herself in the evenings. When returning home, "it was difficult not to be heard," she explained, laughing. This was the only aspect of the apartment that she claims she would have changed. Had the apartment been organized more conventionally, "maybe it would have helped."

Ms. Moreau described a number of details in the apartments that the designers conceived with children in mind. There was the built-in infant changing table in the parents' bedroom, which offered a number of drawers and was well-used for both Ms. Moreau's younger brothers and eventually her own children (figs. 26, 58). Also bespoke were the wooden treads of the Jean Prouvé–designed stairs leading to the second level of the apartment (figs. 59–61). The tread was made up of two par-

▲ A double-sided *boîte à provision* (delivery box) and icebox allowed food, newspapers and ice to be delivered directly into each apartment from the hallway. **[28, 29]**
▼ A model by Le Corbusier showing the relationship of the structural frame and the infilled units. **[30]**

allel pieces of wood with a small gap in the middle large enough for fingers, intended to help little ones crawl up the steps. The stair itself had two different balustrades: a taller one on the wall for adults, and on the open side, a double banister that children of different heights could easily hold onto while climbing up.

Every apartment in the Unité, regardless of size, originally had the same kitchen: it was "very small but very modern for the time," according to Ms. Moreau (fig. 27). "It was designed by Charlotte Perriand, and my mother said, 'You can imagine a woman designed it because you have everything easily at hand.'" When they first moved in, the features of the kitchen did appear futuristic, especially to Gisèle's mother, though she says she herself "was too young to know about that." The small size was not restrictive; "it never bothered my mother, even when we were numerous here."

The *boîte à provision* (delivery box), an amenity that linked the corridor and each unit and allowed food delivery even when inhabitants weren't home, functioned in the Unité in Marseille for only a few years (figs. 28, 29).[14] Ice was delivered the same way, Ms. Moreau described: "From the outside, the ice man used to put an ice bar straight into the icebox every morning, and it also worked for two, three years, and then people started buying fridges. But I remember that very well, very clearly." These aspects, though not functional in the long run, speak to Le Corbusier's ambition to provide amenities for the Unité's inhabitants. "I always say that it was a kind of utopia, because it didn't really work," Ms. Moreau said.

To Ms. Moreau, the sound separation between units in the Unité is very successful. As the famous photograph of a hand inserting a module into a model of the building shows (fig. 30), each apartment exists as a self-contained insert into the robust concrete frame.[15] Accustomed to wearing shoes in the apartment and not worrying about noise, Ms. Moreau learned about the need for slippers only when living in an "ordinary house," after her neighbors complained.

Noise has become an issue in the Unité in recent decades, however, as parents have begun to allow their children to play in the hallways—a practice that was not condoned by previous generations of inhabitants (fig. 63). "Of course, when I was a kid, it was completely forbidden to play 'dans la rue'—in the corridors that we called the streets," Ms. Moreau said. "It was completely forbidden to be in the corridor, because Le Corbusier, I'm sure of that ... Le Corbusier designed them as very dark places because it was supposed to be the transition between the very bright light here [in Marseille] and the quietness of the flat. If he had wanted people to stay and the children to play, he would have made them brighter." She knows that she disagrees with younger parents, including her own daughter, in this respect: "So I didn't play in the corridor, my children didn't play in the corridor, but my grandchildren did play in the corridor!" The resulting sounds do reach Ms. Moreau's unit, a situation not helped by the recent removal of the small entrance vestibule, with its second door, a renovation Ms. Moreau carried out against the advice of her late husband.

When Ms. Moreau was young, children in the Unité—banished from the hallways as they were—commandeered the generous stairwells of the building: "We played in the staircases. We did what we wanted." She remembers games of hide-and-seek there (though the roof and the back of the building also provided good opportunities to hide). These spaces are indeed well-lit and ventilated, in contrast to the dim interior "streets" (figs. 64, 65). The staircases are also the only access points for many social gathering spaces on the floors between the skip-stop corridors, including a film club, library, and art room, where Ms. Moreau still takes painting classes. Another significant communal space was the nursery school run by Lilette Ripert (Madame Ougier), a friend of Gisèle's mother and also a friend of Le Corbusier's and a strong advocate of the building (fig. 31). The educator introduced the children to art, drawing, and music in spaces specifically designed by the architect for this purpose. Le Corbusier "designed the school for her, in fact," Ms. Moreau said.[16]

▼ Lilette Ripert and her students in the rooftop nursery school pavilion. **[31, 32]**

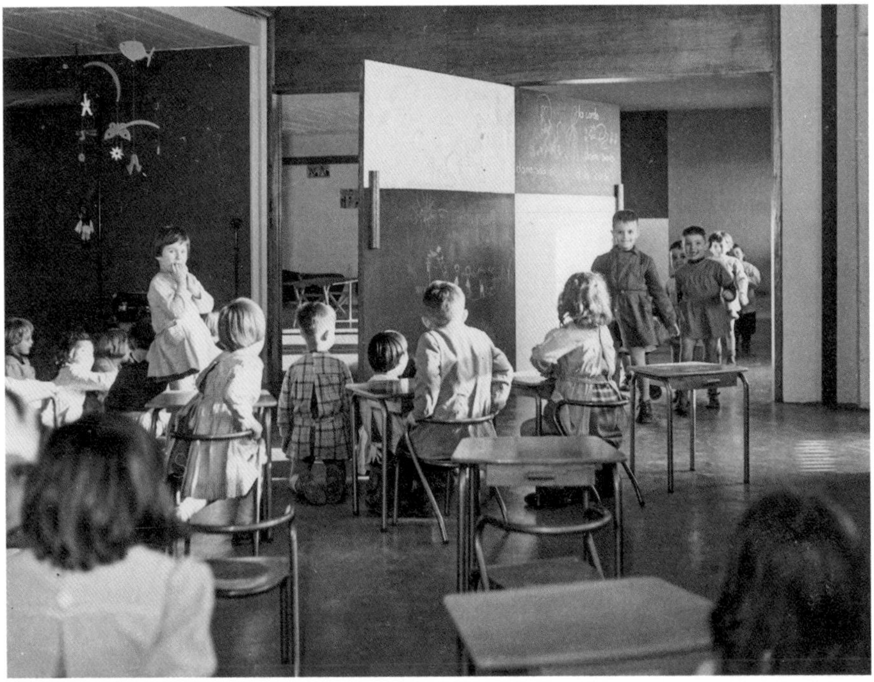

▲ Pupils in Lilette Ripert's primary school on the seventeenth floor of the Unité, just below the roof terrace. [33]

While Gisèle did not attend the school, her younger brothers, her two daughters, and one of her grandchildren did (figs. 32, 33).

In general, there was a feeling of freedom for the children of the Unité during Ms. Moreau's childhood. Compared to friends living elsewhere, who had to ask permission to go to visit others, she remembers a marked sense of independence and safety. "I felt very much freeer here," Ms. Moreau recalled. "And my elder daughter, who lived here for twenty-five years, keeps saying, 'It's paradise for children!'"

Describing the infamous shopping streets of the Unité, Ms. Moreau recalled, "When I was a kid there were shops all over the place on the third floor and a few on the fourth floor, all sorts of shops, and this is where we went shopping every day … . And then maybe ten years after, at the beginning of the sixties, the first supermarket opened here next door [in the neighborhood] and it's still here. So people started going there and little by little, the small shops started to close down. But it was very lively, the third floor was very lively. Few people remember that here." When we visited in 2015, there were still several small stores open, including a bookstore and a small café and gift store, but these appear to cater more to architecture-enthusiast visitors than to the residents of the building, and the liveliness that Ms. Moreau remembers is a thing of the past. "There is a baker, he is probably going to close soon … . Oh, I can't even tell you, there were lots and lots and lots of shops on the third and fourth floors," she said (figs. 66, 67).

When the Unité was first completed, the citizens of Marseille did not appreciate the structure. "Some people found it very ugly when it was being built," Ms. Moreau said. "Maybe I was too young, so I didn't have an opinion, but I have never found it ugly." The building was nicknamed *"la maison du fada"*—crazy house[17]—and the moniker has persisted to this day. Ms. Moreau and other inhabitants don't mind, as the term *fada* in the Provençal dialect can also mean "touched by fairies," and many do find the building magical, as both a piece of architecture and a place to live. "I understood when I was young that it was different and more original than traditional buildings. I'm sure of that," she said.

The Unité is the embodiment of an idea of the collective "that is so precious about Le Corbusier in today's society," Ms. Moreau said. "If you want to be by yourself and get affected by no one, you can. But as I told you, it's the best place for bachelors, widows, widowers … I think! Because it's easy to meet people. There are so many people. And things get organized and you have opportunities to meet people. Yes, yes. It still works. Not as it used to be, but there are enough people who want to keep Le Corbusier's spirit, you know!" According to Ms. Moreau, the Unité and its arrangements of units and communal spaces influence the way that neighbors behave. The architecture gives people "the opportunity to be helpful to their

neighbors, when somebody is sick or out of hospital ... somebody visits him or her, bringing food and being worried about him or her." "In this way, maybe, it improves people. It gives them the opportunity to realize that they can be helpful," she added.

Ms. Moreau believes that the Unité in Marseille is the "most beautiful" of the series of apartment blocks constructed by Le Corbusier: "It's because they spent a fortune on it, and for the other ones there wasn't as much money." She has visited a number of the other Unité buildings and is familiar with not only how they look, but also how they are used—and it is in this respect that she finds the Unité has changed most significantly. "I say that the spirit of Le Corbusier is not in Marseille, it is in Nantes, because they still live in the way that he suggested," she explained. "They [have kept] the cultural center, the social housing, and they have workshops. Everything is free there."

◀ Stills from Gisèle Moreau's conversation with the authors, 2015. **[34]**

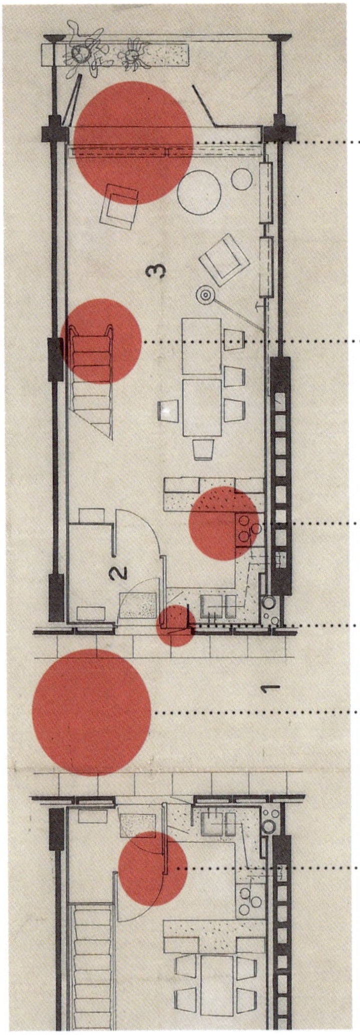

Loggia doors, which Gisèle's mother would keep open for much of the year: "My mother used to open the four windows in May and close them in October." (figs. 22, 44–48)

Internal stairs, which make the apartment seem like a house, according to Ms. Moreau (figs. 49, 59–61)

The "very modern kitchen," one of the amenities much appreciated by Gisèle's mother (figs. 27, 50)

Ice box and a delivery box, which could be accessed from both the hallway and the apartment to allow for delivery of blocks of ice and groceries without disturbing the residents (figs. 28, 29)

Hallway ("interior street"): children were not allowed to play in the hallway when Ms. Moreau was a child, so they commandeered the staircases instead (fig. 63)

Apartment across the hall: "My best friend moved the day before, it was a Tuesday, and for me it was a Wednesday ... We were of the same age and I still see her regularly," Ms. Moreau said

▲▶ Lower-level (above) and upper-level (opposite) apartment plans annotated with references to Ms. Moreau's memories. **[35, 36]**

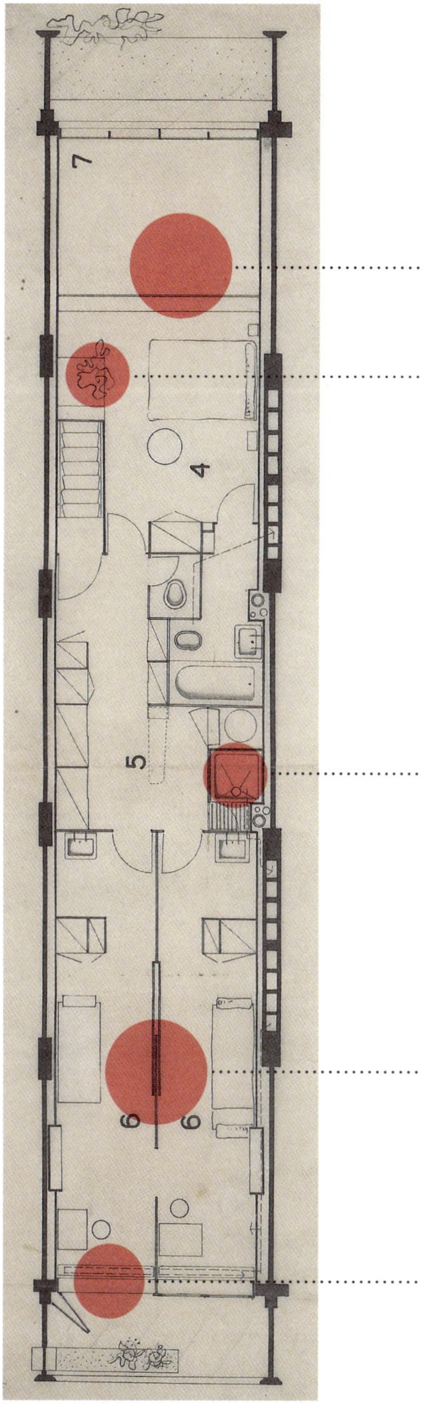

Mezzanine level, where Gisèle's parents' bedroom was located; its openness to the living room below made it difficult when she was a teenager to return after curfew unnoticed (figs. 49, 53)

Built-in infant changing table, used for Gisèle's brothers and later by her to change her own babies (figs. 26, 58)

Children's shower, one of the amenities that most impressed Gisèle's mother and made her want to move into the building (figs. 25, 57)

Sliding blackboard partition, which Gisèle used as a child and all the way through her university studies (figs. 24, 55, 56)

Access to the children's loggia, which was kept open much of the year and provides cross ventilation to the apartment (figs. 23, 54)

◀◀▶ The Unité d'Habitation apartment block seen from the east, photographed in 2015. Gisèle Moreau and her family were among the original inhabitants of the building. [37–39]

◄◄ A view looking up the east facade of the apartment block, showing the colorful awnings and balcony walls and the distinct, vertical concrete brise-soleil of the shopping street. **[40]**

▲ The municipal park and playground to the west of the building. **[41]**

► The entrance canopy and vestibule on the building's east side. **[42]**

▲ The porous base of the building, with the concrete pilotis lifting the structure off the ground. **[43]**

▶ A view looking up the west facade, showing the layering of the double-height and single-height balconies of the skip-stop apartments. Ms. Moreau's double-height balcony off her living room is visible below the brise-soleil of the shopping street, with a plant in the corner. **[44]**

▲ The living room balcony of Ms. Moreau's apartment. **[45]**
► Having lived in several units in the Unité with only a brief time away, Ms. Moreau is now back in the apartment that her family first moved into in 1953. **[46]**

CUIR

◄ Ms. Moreau recalls that her mother would open the balcony doors in May and close them in October so that the balcony became an extension of the living space, as there was very little traffic at the time. **[47]**

▲ Ms. Moreau continues the practice herself, but does close the doors occasionally because of traffic noise. **[48]**

▲ A view of the double-height living space looking back toward the entrance and kitchen, with the master bedroom on the open mezzanine above. As a teenager, Gisèle bemoaned the arrangement, which did not conceal the sounds of her coming home later than expected. **[49]**
▶ Ms. Moreau recently had her kitchen remodeled, keeping the basic arrangement of Charlotte Perriand's original design and some of the details (such as the wood handles of the upper cabinets) but eschewing the original color scheme and material palette. **[50]**

◀◀ A view down to the living room from the mezzanine above. [51]

▲ The hall connecting the parents' sleeping area and those of the children. [52]
▶ The parents' bedroom on the mezzanine, now Ms. Moreau's. [53]

◄◄ The upstairs sitting room in Ms. Moreau's apartment was formerly subdivided in two and served as the children's bedrooms. The skip-stop configuration of the units allows generous cross ventilation. [54]

◄ The two original, narrow children's bedrooms in an empty apartment in the Unité. [55]
▲ The children's rooms are subdivided by a sliding chalkboard, which Ms. Moreau remembers using as a child and all the way through her university studies. [56]

◀ The rounded, ship-like doorway to the children's shower. **[57]**
▲ In the master bedroom, near the vertical grill in the mezzanine guard, was a built-in changing table for babies. Ms. Moreau's mother used it for her brothers, both born in the Unité, and later Ms. Moreau used it for her own daughters. **[58]**

▲ Jean Prouvé designed the interior staircases for the Unité apartments. The gaps in the wooden treads were there to help small children climb the stairs by providing a space for their fingers to grip. **[59]**

▶ The stair had two balustrades: one fixed to the wall, for adults, and the freestanding double banister, which children of different heights could easily hold onto while climbing up. **[60]**

◄ The original color scheme of the various interior elements is visible in the empty apartment, in contrast to Ms. Moreau's recent, more muted remodeling. **[61]**
▲ A view outside through the balcony of the living space. Over the years many more towers and apartment blocks have been constructed in the area. During Gisèle's childhood, there were still several farms in its vicinity, which she would visit daily to fetch milk. **[62]**

◄◄ An interior hallway. The original delivery boxes for groceries for each apartment are visible as blue protrusions near each entry; the small doors directly below once provided access to each unit's icebox. When Gisèle was small, children were not allowed to play in the hallways. **[63]**

◄▲ Barred from the "interior streets," the youngsters in Gisèle's generation and several that followed commandeered the stairways as a place for play. The stairwells were generously daylit from the facade directly on one side and through borrowed daylight from the social programs on the other, making these spaces more amenable to play. **[64, 65]**

▲ The interior shopping streets on the third and fourth levels of the Unité were very active in the decades after the building opened. **[66]**
► At present only a handful of smaller businesses remain, catering more to the architectural enthusiasts that tour the building than to the residents themselves. **[67]**

◀▶▶ The rooftop is the Unité's largest social amenity and Ms. Moreau's favorite place in the building. "It's a miracle," she says. "I still get a shock when the elevator opens and I see the sky and the sea, and it's great! I spent part of my life there looking after my brothers, my two daughters, my four grandchildren. And I picnicked in the evening and I studied my lessons and we played." **[68–70]**

▲ The amorphous concrete rock where Gisèle was sunbathing with a friend and listening to the radio when she learned of the death of Le Corbusier. She was shaken by the news, as she identifies with the architect and the building in a very personal way. **[71]**
► The low partitions offer some privacy, especially welcome now that the building attracts so many visitors. Residents still picnic here, particularly on warm summer evenings. **[72]**

►► The rooftop gymnasium recently became an art gallery, with exhibitions focused on contemporary art and design. Through some residents are not in favor of this use, Ms. Moreau thinks that it adds to the building's many programs and amenities. **[73]**

Notes

1 According to the architect, there was a need for four million dwellings. Le Corbusier, *The Marseilles Block*, trans. Geoffrey Sainsbury (London: Harvill, 1953), 7.

2 Le Corbusier went on to complete Unité Blocks in Rezé-les-Nantes (1955), Berlin (1957), Briey-en-Forêt (1963) and Firminy (1967). For recent documentation of all five Unité projects, see ed. Peter Ottmann, *Le Corbusier: 5 × Unité: Marseille, Nantes, Berlin, Briey, Firminy* (Leipzig: Spector Books, 2019).

3 Robert Furneaux Jordan, *Le Corbusier* (New York: Lawrence Hill, 1972), 79.

4 Jacques Sbriglio, *The Unité d'Habitation in Marseilles: And the Four Other Unité Blocks in Rezé-les-Nantes, Berlin, Briey en Forêt and Firminy* (Paris: Fondation Le Corbusier; Basel: Birkhäuser, 2004), 228.

5 Le Corbusier, *Marseilles Block*, 7.

6 Arguing for the amenities within the project, Le Corbusier wrote, "In the Americas the bathroom is in daily use. Like the motor-car it has become so common that it is well on the way to being an indispensable domestic adjunct. It is necessary to point this out for the benefit of those who think we are proposing a journey to Utopia. We are not. We are simply talking about ROOMS." *Marseilles Block*, 18.

7 Furneaux Jordan describes both the development of the Modulor system by Le Corbusier during the years of World War II and its application in the Unité in Marseille in *Le Corbusier*, 106–27. Perhaps as an antidote to the universalizing principle of the Modulor in his own writing about the Unité, Le Corbusier clearly proves that he was aware of the different sizes of individuals when he describes the seven different age groups of people who would occupy the building and their respective needs. *Marseilles Block*, 25.

8 In 1956, the apartments were sold to the individual occupants.

9 For a discussion of the relationship between the work of Le Corbusier and later French housing projects, see Kenny Cupers, "The Power of Association: Le Corbusier and the *banlieues*," in *Terms of Appropriation: Modern Architecture and Global Exchange*, eds. Amanda Reeser Lawrence and Ana Miljački (Abingdon, UK: Routledge, 2017).

10 Roger Sherwood, *Modern Housing Prototypes* (Cambridge, MA: Harvard University Press, 1978), 125. Sherwood is playing on the words of historian Lewis Mumford, who called the Unité a "monument brilliantly disguised as a housing project."

11 In fact, one of Gisèle's brothers was only the second child to be born to a Unité family—a small pity, in her opinion, because Le Corbusier promised to be the godfather of the first-born baby.

12 With every corner of the apartment in heavy use when she was a child, there was no room for pets in the family, Ms. Moreau explained, but her own daughters wanted a cat, "so we had a cat for seventeen years here."

13 In her recent renovation of the unit, the two bedrooms have been joined into one space, a sitting room (fig. 54).

14 In contrast, at the Unité in Rezé (near Nantes), the delivery box functioned for fifteen years.

15 In his "Description of the Marseilles Block," André Wogenscky explained that the units are inserted into the concrete framework without touching each other; he also noted how "between their floors and the concrete beams which carry them are lead pads which absorb vibrations." In Le Corbusier, *Marseilles Block*, 54.

16 Le Corbusier's ideas about designing learning spaces for children are elaborated in Le Corbusier, *The Nursery Schools*, trans. Eleanor Levieux (New York: Orion Press, 1968).

17 Geoffrey Sainsbury translated the term as "Loony Bin" (Le Corbusier, *Marseilles Block*, 12), while Jacques Sbriglio calls it the "Mad Hatter's House" (*Unité d'Habitation in Marseilles*, 179).

Lessons from Childhoods in Iconic Homes

Conclusion

We have all had childhoods, an obvious but significant fact that has driven our interest in the complex relationships around the Modernist childhood dwelling. As children, we have very little influence over where and how we live—we are thrust into a particular time and place by our parents, and more broadly by larger sociocultural circumstances. In a time when we start to form our ideas about the world and of our own place in it, we are, in fact, in control of little. The homes we inhabit are an embodiment of our individual and collective upbringing; as both outcomes of and triggers for the conditions of our lives, they are a nexus of our circumstances. Similarly, privilege, or lack thereof, is a byproduct of chance and the result of overlapping histories, both personal and global. This was the case for the individuals we spoke with for this book, individuals who, through the choices of their parents, were among the first to dwell in significant Modernist architecture.

The conversations we had pointed to no uniform conclusion, no consistent takeaway (nor universal love of white stucco walls and flat roofs). To attempt to define one single lesson would be much too simplistic and deny the richness of our interactions and the uniqueness of each narrator's circumstances. Nevertheless, these interviews did yield knowledge that might benefit students and designers as much as historians.

Rolf Fassbaender's happy childhood in a row house in the Weissenhof Estate had a lot to do with the proximity of other families with children and the spaces of the estate, which allowed freedom of play.[1] The variety of types of houses and housing in the community, calibrated by Ludwig Mies van der Rohe to respond to the different financial statuses of its inhabitants, led to a balance between built-up and open space in young Rolf's environment. Designed by J.J.P. Oud, the row house itself was compact in area but generous as a dwelling, providing a plethora of amenities for 1927, including indoor plumbing, central heating, a state-of-the-art kitchen, and abundant built-in storage. What stood out were the connections between inside and outside spaces of the dwelling, and the garden in particular. Daylight poured in through large windows and through the milk-glass skylight above the stair and bathroom. Oud took advantage of opportunities on the garden facade, using the entrance canopy as the base of a balcony and placing a concrete bench in the space in front of the living room windows. Both of these moves required extra thought; they are evidence of care and humanism in the architect's approach, an empathy and a sincere desire to provide for the inhabitants.

At eight years old, Ernst Tugendhat was the youngest of our interlocutors when he and his family left the famous Modernist home of his childhood. It is perhaps not surprising, then, that he has the fewest memories of the home's interiors and features. Given the impending invasion by Nazi forces, the circumstances of the relocation must have been deeply emotional and even traumatic, if not for him directly then for the family generally. Coincidentally or consequently, the time he spent in Brno has largely disappeared from Mr. Tugendhat's mind. In its place is not only an aversion to the house itself, but also a general ambivalence toward architecture and design. The lack of emotion that the dwelling elicits in this former inhabitant is tied to his embarrassment about the opulence of the house. His indifference was striking, and one of the biggest surprises of the project for us, as designers indoctrinated through our own architectural education: that someone could grow up in one of history's most famous buildings, designed by a widely acclaimed architect, and not care about it in the slightest. We especially appreciated and welcomed Mr. Tugendhat's frankness, which gave us pause and valuable perspective. Mr. Tugendhat's feelings are unexpected considering the affection that his parents, the clients, professed for the house even well after the family left it. Grete Tugendhat wrote that it allowed them to "feel free to an extent never experienced before";[2] in 1969, during a speech in Brno, she confirmed that she and her husband "loved the house from the very first moment."[3] The freedom the adults experienced in the house was something they anticipated would extend to their children. On February 29, 2012, when the Tugendhat House reopened after an extensive renovation, Daniela Hammer-Tugendhat—the youngest daughter of the Tugendhats, an art historian, and a devoted advocate of the preservation of the house[4]—spoke to these expectations: "My father believed that the beauty and clear forms of the architecture would affect the ethos of the people living in the house and the children growing up there."[5] Fritz Tugendhat may not have guessed exactly how the dwelling would affect his children, nor could he anticipate the course that global history would take.

Helga Zumpfe's personal experience was very different, and her relationship to her childhood home, the Schminke House, stands in sharp contrast to that of Mr. Tugendhat. Even during World War II, she was able to enjoy the home that Hans Scharoun designed for her family in relative safety and comfort. Not only did she live much longer—fifteen years—in the house, at eighteen years old, she was also much older when she left it, so it follows that her memories are stronger and more vivid. While particular features and architectural details play a key role in the stories she tells about the home, it is the building's openness and spaciousness that had the most lasting impression on her, and by extension on us. She internalized these qualities to such an extent that her dreams often still take place inside the house, which after seven decades away is in and of itself remarkable. Further, she has tried to adapt her current living conditions—at least as much as possible, considering her more limited resources—to emulate the openness of the childhood home, privileging views and replacing doors with curtains. Lastly, she convinced her congregation to commission Scharoun to design a church and community space in Bochum, rekindling her relationship with the architect and bringing his architectural approach back into her life.

Having lived for most of her life in the Unité d'Habitation in Marseille, Gisèle Moreau is unique among our narrators. She has been a witness to the building in every era of its existence, and the mythology of the place has become a strong part of her personal story. The identity of the Unité, and by extension the identity of the architect, have over the years become intertwined with her own. She is an advocate for the building and a believer in the goals that Le Corbusier outlined for it. While her parents may have chosen to move into the building in the first place, it is explicitly by choice that Ms. Moreau has stayed there throughout her adulthood. Her emotional attachment was clear when she spoke about the apartment block and how it has changed over time. While the Unité functioned as state-run social housing only in its initial years, it does provide social infrastructures that are essential to its inhabitants, and these in turn enable a strong sense of community. The aspects of community and collective amenity that Le Corbusier embedded into the building are chief among her memories as a child and experiences as an adult.

All of these buildings provided amenities to their inhabitants that we now consider commonplace but were not so at the time of construction. These include indoor plumbing and hot water, purpose-built ergonomic kitchens, and access to

daylight and ventilation. Modernists fought for these conveniences, and especially in the case of housing, these battles were not apolitical. For example, the fact that the city's water supply was not immediately connected to Le Corbusier's Cité Frugès development, in Pessac, forcing it to languish vacant for three years after its construction, was not a coincidence; rather, it demonstrated how the higher echelons of society exerted control over the circumstances of the working class.[6] The wonder Ms. Moreau's mother expressed at the conveniences in the Unité is proof that even in the 1950s, these everyday services were not ubiquitous—they were luxuries. Architects' investment in the modernization of the dwelling, a basic but significant victory of Modernism, should not be taken for granted.

Similarly, the spatial organization of each home reflects not only the client's wishes, but also the architect's agenda; in some instances, the layout speaks to broader societal shifts as well. While the traditional separation between living and service spaces persists in both the Tugendhat House and the Schminke House, for example,[7] one notices a clear difference between the place of the children in family dynamics in the two villas: in the Tugendhat House, the children's bedrooms and dedicated terrace are all located upstairs (a dumbwaiter delivered their suppers upstairs),[8] while in the Schminke House, the children were emphatically at the heart of the home. Connections between the kitchen and living spaces may have dissolved gender roles, too: in the Oud row house, with the pass-through Mr. Fassbaender recalls so well, and later in Le Corbusier's Unité, where the kitchen was open and integral to the living spaces of the apartment.

In listening to our interlocutors' stories about these important examples of Modernism, we were most struck by how the moments of humanism in the architecture play out in the memories of those who inhabited these spaces. At the scale of a building, for example, the rooftop of the Unité—a significant social amenity—serves to this day as a place of relief and play, just as the architect intended (fig. 1). Organizationally, locating the playroom at the center of the building in the Schminke House enabled and empowered the children in the home. The pass-through from the kitchen to the dining area of the Oud row house shaped family interactions, just as the playroom's wide windowsill at the Schminke House, with its conspicuously adjacent operable pane, allowed the kids direct access outside before they could even reach a door handle. It is the details, designed for utility but also beauty, that endure in inhabitants' minds: the colorful glass portholes of the Schminke House, or the balcony and bench of the Oud row house. Designers and

◀ At the Unité d'Habitation in Marseille, the rooftop wading pool offered welcome relief from a heat wave during our stay. [1]
▼ In conversation with Helga Zumpfe about her memories of her childhood in the Schminke House. Like many of our interlocutors, she welcomed us into her home and graciously humored the presence of our son. [2]

▲ We enjoyed the living spaces of the Schminke House before visitors returned for afternoon tours. [3]

students of architecture history must be aware of not only the utilitarian amenities adopted as standard under Modernism, but also the particular generosity that was a feature of at least some of the early examples of the movement. While the lessons of Modernism's focus on efficiency have made their way into the housing canon over the last century, its humanist aspirations and social agendas, at both the individual and collective scales, have often been backgrounded. There is no doubt that specific, humane design requires inventiveness and care on the part of the architect; it often, but not always, requires an additional financial investment. Based on our conversations, we have come to believe it is precisely the moments where such thought is evident that endear buildings to people.

These are significant lessons as we deepen our understanding of Modernists' audacity in questioning conventions and defying norms. A boldness and belief in architecture as a vehicle for creating a modern society is present in all the buildings presented in this book. One might question whether architecture can still assert such a powerful agenda today. One could also argue that in a world quickly succumbing to climate crisis, architects need to take up this level of agency and ambition once again. This will happen not through stylistic exploration, but through a broader reconsideration of the amenity of building today—how architecture can provide not just established basics, but also social empowerment and environmental resourcefulness. Perhaps these battles need to be fought at a scale larger than individual houses, but there is no doubt that a societal shift is necessary and that architecture needs to respond to this new zeitgeist.

Modernism was undoubtedly affected by World War II, and any history of the movement needs to acknowledge the war's immediate and long-term consequences. The violence and trauma of the war touched our narrators personally and changed the courses of their lives, directly or indirectly. Without the rise of the National Socialists, the war, and its aftermath, Mr. Tugendhat would have likely stayed in his childhood home longer, while Ms. Moreau may not have had the chance to live in the Unité at all.[9] While the looming effects of the war on our interlocutors were apparent, in our conversations we did not tease out specific details related to this aspect of their personal histories. Immensely appreciative of the generosity of the individuals we spoke with, we were timid to ask direct questions about the war and its role in their lives. This lacuna is a weakness of this study, but it is also a byproduct of the way in which the conversations were held—in intimate private homes, devoid of the sterile objectivity of an academic setting. It is also a byproduct of who we are as individuals and the comfort we wished to maintain during the conversations (for both parties). To quote Naomi Stead: "All scholars are influenced by the particularities of their backgrounds and education, plus the identity categories of class, race, and gender, plus the irrationalities of their emotions, but also their own bodies—we write and speak not only as disembodied floating brains, but as bodies with needs and wants of their own."[10]

To conduct the interviews for this project, we traveled around Europe in a camper van—an *Existenzminimum* dwelling in and of itself—through a heat wave, with our child, who was just learning to stand on his own two legs (figs. 2–6).[11] The fragility of our son's balance was a good reminder of the growing and changing child's body, while his demands for food and sleep ruled our schedule as much as the interview appointments did. Each of the conversations took place under different circumstances, and we personally learned from each, beyond the content of the

◀ Visiting the Tugendhat House: with our son by the terrace stair (top), in the living room (center), and in the winter garden (bottom). [4–6]
▲ An interview with Mr. and Mrs. Goron, inhabitants of the Le Corbusier–designed Cité Frugès, in Pessac, near Bordeaux. Several of the conversations we had for the project were not included in this book, but all were instructive and insightful. [7]

stories the narrators shared about their childhood homes. We learned how to ask our questions better, how to leave more time for replies, and how not to interrupt the recording with laughter. Navigating language barriers and age differences involved deciphering body language and interpreting social customs. Perhaps having a fussy baby along for the ride helped to make the circumstances familiar or familial, disarming our narrators—or maybe it was a nuisance, though they were all too polite to say so (figs. 2, 7–10).

We have often had to make the case that we are the right people to be doing this research and to be writing this book.[12] We were the ones who had the idea to take the memories of children as inhabitants of Modernism seriously, but was this enough to qualify us for this endeavor? When we embarked on our journey of creative documentation, we were not practiced interviewers, nor were we seasoned photographers. We were not experts in Modernism, historians, psychologists, or oral historians. We were, and we are, simply a couple with backgrounds in architecture and visual arts and interests in spatial history and narrative. We are parents—and as these are children's stories, perhaps this is also relevant.[13] We are de-

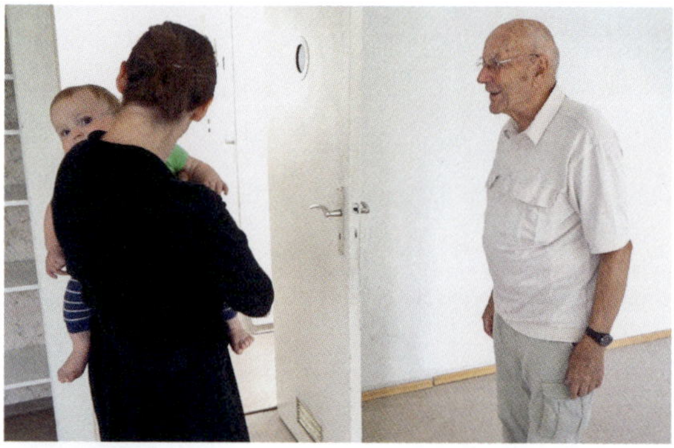

▲ Rolf Fassbaender playing hide-and-seek with our son while showing us the portholes that feature in the interior doors in J. J. P. Oud's Weissenhof Estate row houses. **[8–10]**

▲ Our reflections in the storage cabinets of the nursery in the Tugendhat House. [11]

signers, and we are educators. Perhaps most significantly, we were curious and persistent enough to try to get in contact with these individuals, and through them to add to our knowledge of the icons of Modernism.

We had few conscious preconceptions when we started our research. We were not sure what to expect from our interlocutors and how much or how little they would remember of their pasts in Modernist homes. We hoped their memories would be vivid—but we were aware that because so much time had passed, this was rather unlikely. We were not sure if their recollections would be positive or negative, and the extent to which they would communicate these emotions. We found it deeply endearing that people wanted to speak with us and share their experiences. We left the interviews with genuine gratitude for the time and openness of each interlocutor, for their trust and willingness to talk to us, total strangers, about intimate details of their upbringing. For our part, we believed—and in this we were proven correct—that hearing about the history of a place from someone who grew up there would help us understand the architecture better and would make us pay attention to it in a different way. This, too, may be an obvious but significant fact, but one that the discipline of architecture still needs to absorb and put into active practice.

Notes

1 We are careful not to attribute a child's happiness to the home where he or she grew up; clearly the causality is much more complicated. While it is fair to state that Oud's design only added to Mr. Fassbaender's happy childhood, it is evident that his happiness is more in debt to the efforts of his mother—which leaves us to wonder if he would have experienced the same level of happiness in an entirely different dwelling.

2 Grete Tugendhat, "The Inhabitants of the Tugendhat House Give Their Opinion," letter to the editor, *Die Form* 6. no 11, November 15, 1931, reprinted and translated in Daniela Hammer-Tugendhat, Ivo Hammer, and Wolf Tegethoff, *Tugendhat House: Ludwig Mies van der Rohe*, new ed. (Basel: Birkhäuser, 2015), 77.

3 Grete Tugendhat, "On the Construction of the Tugendhat House," lecture, Brno House of Arts, January 17, 1969, printed and translated in Hammer-Tugendhat et al., *Tugendhat House*, 21.

4 Daniela was born in 1946 in Caracas, Venezuela, after the family was forced to flee the house in Brno.

5 Daniela Hammer-Tugendhat, "Speech on the Occasion of the Opening of the Tugendhat House in Brno on February 29, 2012," printed in Hammer-Tugendhat et al., *Tugendhat House*, 226.

6 Philippe Boudon, *Lived-In Architecture: Le Corbusier's Pessac Revisited*, trans. Gerald Onn (Cambridge, MA: MIT Press, 1972).

7 In both of these homes these were literally servants' spaces, though Mrs. Zumpfe notes that her mother did take part in preparing meals and the children would also help in the kitchen.

8 While the separation may have been the Tugendhats' wish, it is also very likely that Mies would have questioned this if the organizational strategy and its social implications had been a part of his agenda.

9 It remains an unanswered question in our minds whether Modernism would have thrived as it did without the need for rebuilding after World War II. In the case of the Unité, the commission was a direct response by the government to the housing shortage created by the war.

10 Naomi Stead, "Architectural Affections: On Some Modes of Conversation in Architecture, Towards a Disciplinary Theorisation of Oral History," *Fabrications: The Journal of the Society of Architectural Historians, Australia and New Zealand* 24, no. 2 (2014): 156. Quoted in Janina Gosseye, Naomi Stead, and Deborah van der Plaat, eds., *Speaking of Buildings: Oral History in Architectural Research* (New York: Princeton Architectural Press, 2019), 15.

11 He stood unaided for the first time in the week between our interview with Mrs. Zumpfe and our visit to her childhood home. (He would walk months later in our wooden Victorian home in Buffalo, New York.)

12 This has been a typical question on the applications for grants and awards that we have completed over the course of the project.

13 At the time that we applied for our first grant to support the research, the Lawrence B. Anderson Award, our child had not yet been born.

Acknowledgments

There are many individuals and institutions whom we would like to thank and without whom this publication would not have been possible. We are foremost enormously grateful to the individuals who chose to speak to us about their experiences growing up Modern: Mr. Fassbaender, Mr. Tugendhat, Mrs. Zumpfe, and Ms. Moreau. We are grateful for their patience, their generosity, and their trust. We hope that we have done justice to their stories. We are also grateful to Mr. and Mrs. Goron, residents of the Cité Frugès in Pessac and Mr. Reif, who grew up in a Walter Gropius-designed home on the Weissenhof Estate; while their accounts do not feature prominently here, their personal stories of Modernist homes and neighborhoods gave us new perspectives, and we equally appreciate their time and goodwill.

We are thankful to the institutions and in particular their employees who were supportive of the project and who, in many instances, not only created the connections to our interlocutors, but also provided support later on in the development of the material and answered our continuing questions and queries. They included especially Anja Krämer at the Weissenhofmuseum in Stuttgart and Julia Bojaryn of the Stiftung Haus Schminke in Löbau. Staff members at the Fondation Le Corbusier, especially Bénédicte Gandini, were instrumental in connecting us with a number of individuals who live or have lived in Le Corbusier buildings, including Martine Vittu residing at the Unité in Rezé, with whom we unfortunately did not manage to hold a conversation. A further thank you goes to Cyril Zozor, manager of the Cité Frugès for the City of Pessac, who was generous in setting up a conversation with Mr. and Mrs. Goron. Thanks are also due to Petr Dvořák of the Tugendhat House for allowing us to freely photograph the house.

Colleagues at the University at Buffalo's School of Architecture and Planning, including Beth Tauke, Brian Carter, Joyce Hwang, Despina Stratigakos, and Samina Raja, have been extremely supportive of the endeavor and the intellectual inquiry of this project and have both validated and challenged us along the way. Our gratitude further goes to the former and current Chairs of the Department of Architecture, Omar Khan and Korydon Smith, as well as the Dean of the School, Robert Shibley, for their ongoing support and expanded view of the interconnected nature of research and creative activity in the field of architecture.

A Faculty Fellowship through the Humanities Institute at the University at Buffalo in 2018 offered both time to concentrate on the writing, through a semester-long course release, and valuable peer feedback from the other Fellows. Many thanks to the Institute's Director, David Castillo; Interim Executive Director, Kari Winter; and Program Administrator, Maki Tanigaki.

Parts of the material presented here were initially developed for a micronarrative for the *Journal of Architectural Education* under the title "Growing up Modern – Oral History as Architectural Preservation" (*Journal of Architectural Education* 72, no. 2, "Preserve": 284–89). The feedback of the issue's editors, Ted Shelton and Tricia Stuth; peer reviewers; and the *JAE*'s associate editor, Carolina Dayer, were essential in focusing the larger intellectual framework for the research and compelling us to dive into the material we had gathered in 2015.

A personal narrative based on the material from the "Growing up Modern" research appears in the "Character" issue of *MAS Context*, edited by Iker Gil with issue guest editors Stewart Hicks and Allison Newmeyer. The printed issue came out in 2020, but the initial piece was accepted through an open call in 2016, and we were thrilled to receive the editors' early encouragement.

The research was presented at several academic conferences, including the 2018 Association of Collegiate Schools of Architecture (ACSA) Fall Conference, in Milwaukee, Wisconsin; the 2019 College Art Association's Annual Conference, in New York City; the ACSA's 2020 Annual Meeting, held virtually; and "The Practice of Architectural Research" symposium organized jointly by KU Leuven and the University of Antwerp, held virtually in 2020. The feedback from the audience, panelists, and moderators, especially from Tamar Zinguer, at these events was motivating in the critical development and refinement of the material.

We are further grateful to Eve Kahn, who in 2019 authored an article in the *New York Times* featuring the research project (published on May 6, 2019), giving us exposure to a broader audience and validating the importance of these stories.

This project has been funded by the Lawrence B. Anderson Award, a grant for creative documentation for an alumnus of MIT. We are grateful to the jury, who believed in the initial premise and gave the impetus and necessary funding to begin this research.

This publication was funded through the New York State Council on the Arts's Architecture + Design program, in the Independent Projects category. Thanks to Kristin Herron for her help in sharing the constructive feedback of the jury and administering the grant.

We are equally grateful to Elise Jaffe + Jeffrey Brown for their generous matching support, which truly enabled this publication.

The Architectural League of New York was the fiscal sponsor for both awards, and we appreciate the organization's help, especially that of executive director

Rosalie Genevro and development manager Daniel Cioffi, with the facilitation and administration of the funds, as well as in the promotion of the project.

Sincere thanks to the copyright and authors' rights holders of the historical images used in this book. Many of the photographs and drawings come from institutional and archival collections, but access to most of the material was remote and required the patience and dedication of multiple individuals to locate the material and make it accessible to us, all in the time of the COVID-19 pandemic. In this respect we are especially thankful to Anja Krämer at the Weissenhofmuseum, Julia Bojaryn at the Stiftung Haus Schminke, Isabelle Godineau at the Fondation Le Corbusier, Marie-Noëlle Perrin at the Archives de Marseille, Iris de Jong at Het Nieuwe Instituut, Erika Babatz at the Bauhaus-Archiv, Katja Marciniak and Tanja Morgenstern at the Baukunstarchiv of the Akademie der Künste, Berlin, and Barbora Benčíková of the Study Documentation Centre at the Villa Tugendhat. We are also grateful to Daniela Hammer-Tugendhat for allowing us the use of a few photographs from her personal archive.

On the publisher's side, a sincere thank you to Ria Stein at Birkhäuser for believing in the project and making it a reality; for trusting us, as unseasoned authors, to deliver on our proposal; and for her patience and grace along the way. Genuine thanks to Jayne Kelley for her keen eye and inquisitive insight in copy editing and for tirelessly working with us to reach a balance of tone between the academic and the familiar. Our appreciation goes to Miriam Bussmann for her work on the graphic design, and for being open to our feedback while bringing all her skills to make this book a handsome tactile and visual object.

Many friends and acquaintances have over the years listened to us talk about the research project—thanks to their curiosity, we grew to believe that these stories would be interesting not just to us but also to others, both in and outside the field of architecture. Thank you for those conversations. In addition, we have called on friends for last-minute translations—Zubaida Syed, Christian Zerreis, Hendrik Schikarski, Jordan Geiger, and Miriam Paeslack, thank you for your help.

Lastly, a thank you to our parents, Bożena and Janusz Jamrozik and Janet and Geoff Kempster: we wouldn't be who we are without you. We might not have grown up in Modernism, but with your love and support we certainly did grow up able to choose our own paths, wandering a little along the way.

About the Authors

Julia Jamrozik and Coryn Kempster are designers, artists, and educators. Julia is an Assistant Professor and Coryn is an Adjunct Assistant Professor in the Department of Architecture at the University at Buffalo, the State University of New York. Julia obtained an Honours Bachelor of Arts degree with majors in Architectural Studies and Art History from the University of Toronto and a Master of Architecture from the University of British Columbia in 2007. Coryn holds an Honours Bachelor of Arts from the University of Toronto with majors in Architectural Studies and Visual Studies. He earned his Master of Architecture from the Massachusetts Institute of Technology with a concentration in Visual Arts in 2008.

Between 2008 and 2014, Coryn was an architect at Herzog & de Meuron and a Project Director at Harry Gugger Studio in Basel, Switzerland. Julia also worked as an architect at Herzog & de Meuron and taught architectural design studios at the ETH in Zurich as part of the Gastdozentur of Manuel Herz.

They collaborate on projects in different media and at a variety of scales, from temporary installations to permanent public artworks and architectural projects. Their academic research focuses on the role of play in the built environment and alternative methods of documentation as a form of historic preservation. Their multidisciplinary practice, Coryn Kempster Julia Jamrozik, was recognized in 2018 with the League Prize by The Architectural League of New York.

Illustration Credits

Cover	Photo by Coryn Kempster and Julia Jamrozik, 2015

Weissenhof Estate Row House, pp. 18–81

p. 18	Photo by Coryn Kempster and Julia Jamrozik, 2015
Fig. 1	© Strähle Luftbild Schorndorf.
Fig. 2	Photo by Evert van Ojen. Collection Het Nieuwe Instituut/ OUDJ, ph406
Fig. 3	Photo by Evert van Ojen. Collection Het Nieuwe Instituut/ OUDJ, ph408
Fig. 4	Collection Het Nieuwe Instituut/ OUDJ, st17. © 2021 Artists Rights Society (ARS), New York / c/o Pictoright Amsterdam
Fig. 5	Collection Het Nieuwe Instituut/ OUDJ, st40 (detail). © 2021 Artists Rights Society (ARS), New York / c/o Pictoright Amsterdam
Figs. 6, 7	Photos by Coryn Kempster and Julia Jamrozik, 2015
Figs. 8–10	Photos from Rolf Fassbaender's collection. Courtesy of Weissenhofmuseum
Fig. 11	Photo by Dr. Lossen & Co/Lichtbildgesellschaft, 1927. Bauhaus-Archiv Berlin
Figs. 12–14	Photos from Rolf Fassbaender's collection. Courtesy of Weissenhofmuseum
Figs. 15–19	Photo by Mrs. Wittig, circa 1936. Photo from Rolf Fassbaender's collection. Courtesy of Weissenhofmuseum
Fig. 20	Photo by Coryn Kempster and Julia Jamrozik, 2015
Figs. 21–23	Photos from Rolf Fassbaender's collection. Courtesy of Weissenhofmuseum
Fig. 24	Photo by Evert van Ojen. Collection Het Nieuwe Instituut/ OUDJ, ph414
Fig. 25	Evangelische Gesamtkirchengemeinde Stuttgart
Fig. 26	Photo by Iris Geiger-Messner, 2017. Landesamt für Denkmalpflege im RP Stuttgart
Figs. 27, 28	Photos from Rolf Fassbaender's collection. Courtesy of Weissenhofmuseum
Figs. 29, 30	Photos by Coryn Kempster and Julia Jamrozik, 2015
Figs. 31–33	Diagrams by Julia Jamrozik and Coryn Kempster overlaid on detail from J. J. P. Oud drawing from the Collection Het Nieuwe Instituut/ OUDJ, st40. Drawing © 2021 Artists Rights Society (ARS), New York / c/o Pictoright Amsterdam
Figs. 34–59	Photos by Coryn Kempster and Julia Jamrozik, 2015

Tugendhat House, pp. 82–149

p. 82	Photo by Coryn Kempster and Julia Jamrozik, 2015
Fig. 1	Photo by Studio Rudolf de Sandalo. Daniela Hammer-Tugendhat Archive
Figs. 2, 3	Photos by Studio Rudolf de Sandalo, 1930. Bauhaus-Archiv Berlin
Fig. 4	Tugendhat House, Brno, Czechoslovakia, 1928–30. "Upper-story" plan. Ink on tracing paper, 22 1/4 x 34 1/2". The Mies van der Rohe Archive, the Museum of Modern Art, New York. Gift of the architect. Drawing © ARS, NY. Digital image © The Museum of Modern Art/Licensed by SCALA /Art Resource, NY
Fig. 5	Tugendhat House, Brno, Czechoslovakia, 1928–30. "Ground-floor" plan. Ink, pencil on tracing paper, 24 1/2 x 38 1/2". The Mies van der Rohe Archive, the Museum of Modern Art, New York. Gift of the architect. Drawing © ARS, NY. Digital image © The Museum of Modern Art/Licensed by SCALA /Art Resource, NY
Fig. 6	Photo by Coryn Kempster and Julia Jamrozik, 2015
Fig. 7	Photo by Fritz Tugendhat. © Daniela Hammer-Tugendhat Archive
Fig. 8	Photo by Studio Rudolf de Sandalo (?), 1930. Bauhaus-Archiv Berlin
Figs. 9, 10	Photo by Studio Rudolf de Sandalo, 1930. Bauhaus-Archiv Berlin
Fig. 11	Photo by Studio Rudolf de Sandalo, 1931. Brno City Museum. © Rudolf Sandalo Jr.
Figs. 12, 13	Photos by Fritz Tugendhat. © Daniela Hammer-Tugendhat Archive
Figs. 14–16	Photos by Studio Rudolf de Sandalo, 1931. Brno City Museum. © Rudolf Sandalo Jr.
Figs. 17, 18	Photos by Studio Rudolf de Sandalo, 1930. Bauhaus-Archiv Berlin
Fig. 19	Photo by Studio Rudolf de Sandalo (?), 1930–31. Bauhaus-Archiv Berlin

Fig. 20 Photo by Studio Rudolf de Sandalo, 1931. Brno City Museum. © Rudolf Sandalo Jr.
Figs. 21–23 Photos by Coryn Kempster and Julia Jamrozik, 2015
Fig. 24 Diagram by Julia Jamrozik and Coryn Kempster overlaid on drawing by Ludwig Mies van der Rohe. Tugendhat House, Brno, Czechoslovakia, 1928–30. "Upper-story" plan. Ink on tracing paper, 22 1/4 x 34 1/2". The Mies van der Rohe Archive, the Museum of Modern Art, New York. Gift of the architect. Drawing © ARS, NY. Digital image © The Museum of Modern Art/Licensed by SCALA /Art Resource, NY
Fig. 25 Diagram by Julia Jamrozik and Coryn Kempster overlaid on drawing by Ludwig Mies van Der Rohe. Tugendhat House, Brno, Czechoslovakia, 1928–30. "Ground-floor" plan. Ink, pencil on tracing paper, 24 1/2 x 38 1/2". The Mies van der Rohe Archive, the Museum of Modern Art, New York. Gift of the architect. Drawing © ARS, NY. Digital image © The Museum of Modern Art/Licensed by SCALA / Art Resource, NY
Figs. 26–61 Photos by Coryn Kempster and Julia Jamrozik, 2015

Schminke House, pp. 150–231
p. 150 Photo by Coryn Kempster and Julia Jamrozik, 2015
Fig. 1 Photo by Alice Kerling, 1933. Akademie der Künste, Berlin, Hans-Scharoun-Archiv Nr. 3757 F.124/24a
Fig. 2 Photo by Alice Kerling, 1933. Akademie der Künste, Berlin, Hans-Scharoun-Archiv Nr. 3757 F.124/17a
Fig. 3 Photo by Alice Kerling, 1933. Akademie der Künste, Berlin, Hans-Scharoun-Archiv Nr. 3757 F.124/28a
Fig. 4 Photo by Alice Kerling, 1933. Akademie der Künste, Berlin, Hans-Scharoun-Archiv Nr. 3757 F.124/90a
Fig. 5 Photo by Alice Kerling, 1933. Akademie der Künste, Berlin, Hans-Scharoun-Archiv Nr. 3757 F.124/98
Fig. 6 Akademie der Künste, Berlin, Hans-Scharoun-Archiv Nr. 1305 Bl. 124/9
Fig. 7 Akademie der Künste, Berlin, Hans-Scharoun-Archiv Nr. 1305 Bl. 124/3
Fig. 8 Photo by Coryn Kempster and Julia Jamrozik, 2015
Fig. 9 1934 (?). Stiftung Haus Schminke
Fig. 10 Akademie der Künste, Berlin, Hans-Scharoun-Sammlung Nr. 79 F.571
Fig. 11 Akademie der Künste, Berlin, Hans-Scharoun-Sammlung Nr. 79 F.73
Fig. 12 Akademie der Künste, Berlin, Hans-Scharoun-Archiv Nr. 3757 F.124/53
Figs. 13, 14 Photos by Charlotte Schminke (?), 1934. Stiftung Haus Schminke
Figs. 15–17 Photos by Charlotte Schminke (?), Stiftung Haus Schminke
Fig. 18 Akademie der Künste, Berlin, Hans-Scharoun-Sammlung Nr. 79 F.171
Figs. 19, 20 Photos by Coryn Kempster and Julia Jamrozik, 2015
Fig. 21 Akademie der Künste, Berlin, Hans-Scharoun-Sammlung Nr. 79 F.79
Fig. 22 Akademie der Künste, Berlin, Hans-Scharoun-Sammlung Nr. 79 F.1435
Fig. 23 1934 (?). Akademie der Künste, Berlin, Hans-Scharoun-Sammlung Nr. 39 F.91
Fig. 24 Photo by Alice Kerling, 1933. Akademie der Künste, Berlin, Hans-Scharoun-Archiv Nr. 3757 F.124/101
Fig. 25 Akademie der Künste, Berlin, Hans-Scharoun-Sammlung Nr. 79 F.1377
Fig. 26 Akademie der Künste, Berlin, Hans-Scharoun-Sammlung Nr. 79 F.808
Fig. 27 Akademie der Künste, Berlin, Hans-Scharoun-Sammlung Nr. 79 F.810
Fig. 28 Akademie der Künste, Berlin, Hans-Scharoun-Sammlung Nr. 79 F.98
Fig. 29 Akademie der Künste, Berlin, Hans-Scharoun-Sammlung Nr. 79 F.97
Fig. 30 Akademie der Künste, Berlin, Hans-Scharoun-Sammlung Nr. 79 F.265
Fig. 31 Akademie der Künste, Berlin, Hans-Scharoun-Sammlung Nr. 79 F.448
Fig. 32 Photo by Alice Kerling, 1933. Akademie der Künste, Berlin, Hans-Scharoun-Archiv Nr. 3757 F.124/86
Fig. 33 Photo by Charlotte Schminke (?). Stiftung Haus Schminke

Fig. 34	Photos by Alice Kerling, 1933. Akademie der Künste, Berlin, Hans-Scharoun-Archiv Nr. 3757 F.124/112a
Fig. 35	Photo by Alice Kerling, 1933. Akademie der Künste, Berlin, Hans-Scharoun-Archiv Nr. 3757 F.124/111a
Fig. 36	Akademie der Künste, Berlin, Hans-Scharoun-Sammlung Nr. 79 F.169
Fig. 37	1934 (?). Stiftung Haus Schminke
Figs. 38–40	Photos by Coryn Kempster and Julia Jamrozik, 2015
Fig. 41	Diagram by Julia Jamrozik and Coryn Kempster overlaid on drawing by Laurence Pattacini (based on drawing of the reconstruction of the Schminke House garden by Claudia Feltrup, 1992)
Fig. 42	Diagram by Julia Jamrozik and Coryn Kempster overlaid on drawing by Hans Scharoun. Drawing from the Akademie der Künste, Berlin, Hans-Scharoun-Archiv Nr. 1305 Bl.124/9
Fig. 43	Diagram by Julia Jamrozik and Coryn Kempster overlaid on drawing by Hans Scharoun. Drawing from the Akademie der Künste, Berlin, Hans-Scharoun-Archiv Nr.1305 Bl.124/3
Figs. 44–81	Photos by Coryn Kempster and Julia Jamrozik, 2015

Unité d'Habitation, pp. 232–305

p. 232	Photo by Coryn Kempster and Julia Jamrozik, 2015
Fig. 1	Photo by Ets Jules Richard. Fondation Le Corbusier, L1(13)5. © F.L.C. / ADAGP, Paris / Artists Rights Society (ARS), New York 2021
Fig. 2	Photo by Louis Sciarli. Fondation Le Corbusier (Archives départementales des Bouches-du-Rhône), L1(11)1. © F.L.C. / ADAGP, Paris / Artists Rights Society (ARS), New York 2021
Fig. 3	Fondation Le Corbusier, Plan FLC 25241A. © F.L.C. / ADAGP, Paris / Artists Rights Society (ARS), New York 2021
Fig. 4	Le Corbusier, L'Unité d'habitation de Marseille, Le Point, 1950. Fondation Le Corbusier. © F.L.C. / ADAGP, Paris / Artists Rights Society (ARS), New York 2021
Fig. 5	Le Corbusier, *Œuvre Complète*, volume 5, 1946–1952, p. 194. Fondation Le Corbusier. © F.L.C. / ADAGP, Paris / Artists Rights Society (ARS), New York 2021
Fig. 6	Fondation Le Corbusier, Plan FLC 29364. © F.L.C. / ADAGP, Paris / Artists Rights Society (ARS), New York 2021. Grey highlight by authors
Fig. 7	Fondation Le Corbusier, Plan FLC 26827. © F.L.C. / ADAGP, Paris / Artists Rights Society (ARS), New York 2021. Grey highlight by authors
Fig. 8	Photo by Coryn Kempster and Julia Jamrozik, 2015
Fig. 9	Photo by Louis Sciarli, 1951. Archives de Marseille/Louis Sciarli 47 Fi 108
Fig. 10	ARC: 19987949, U.S. National Archives
Fig. 11	Photo by Louis Sciarli, 1953. Archives de Marseille/Louis Sciarli 47 Fi 534
Fig. 12	Photo by Louis Sciarli, 1953. Archives de Marseille/Louis Sciarli 47 Fi 540
Fig. 13	Photo by Louis Sciarli, 1953. Archives de Marseille/Louis Sciarli 47 Fi 1256
Fig. 14	Photo by Louis Sciarli, 1953. Archives de Marseille/Louis Sciarli 47 Fi 1236
Fig. 15	Photo by Louis Sciarli, 1953. Archives de Marseille/Louis Sciarli 47 Fi 1075
Fig. 16	Photo by Louis Sciarli. Fondation Le Corbusier (Archives départementales des Bouches-du-Rhône), L1(11)12. © F.L.C. / ADAGP, Paris / Artists Rights Society (ARS), New York 2021
Fig. 17	Photo by Louis Sciarli. Fondation Le Corbusier (Archives départementales des Bouches-du-Rhône), L1(11)43. © F.L.C. / ADAGP, Paris / Artists Rights Society (ARS), New York 2021
Fig. 18	Photo by Louis Sciarli. Fondation Le Corbusier (Archives départementales des Bouches-du-Rhône), L1(11)46. © F.L.C. / ADAGP, Paris / Artists Rights Society (ARS), New York 2021
Fig. 19	Photo by Louis Sciarli, 1953. Archives de Marseille/Louis Sciarli 47 Fi 545
Figs. 20–22	Photos by René Burri, 1959. © Magnum Photos
Fig. 23	Photo by Photographie Industrielle du Sud-Ouest, 1949. Fondation Le Corbusier, L1(15)27. © F.L.C. / ADAGP, Paris / Artists Rights Society (ARS), New York 2021
Fig. 24	Photo by Photographie Industrielle du Sud-Ouest, 1949. Fondation Le Corbusier, L1(15)62. © F.L.C. / ADAGP, Paris / Artists Rights Society (ARS), New York 2021

Fig. 25 Photo by Louis Sciarli, 1953. Archives de Marseille/Louis Sciarli 47 Fi 492
Fig. 26 Photo by Louis Sciarli, 1953. Archives de Marseille/Louis Sciarli 47 Fi 507
Fig. 27 Photo by Louis Sciarli, 1953. Archives de Marseille/Louis Sciarli 47 Fi 511
Fig. 28 Photo by Louis Sciarli, 1953. Archives de Marseille/Louis Sciarli 47 Fi 552
Fig. 29 Photo by Louis Sciarli, 1953. Archives de Marseille/Louis Sciarli 47 Fi 537
Fig. 30 Photo by Robert Doisneau. Fondation Le Corbusier, L1(12)54. © F.L.C. / ADAGP, Paris / Artists Rights Society (ARS), New York 2021
Fig. 31 Photo by Louis Sciarli, 1953. Archives de Marseille/Louis Sciarli 47 Fi 488
Fig. 32 Photo by Louis Sciarli, 1953. Archives de Marseille/Louis Sciarli 47 Fi 1080
Fig. 33 Photo by Louis Sciarli. Fondation Le Corbusier, L1(11)71. © F.L.C. / ADAGP, Paris / Artists Rights Society (ARS), New York 2021
Fig. 34 Photo by Coryn Kempster and Julia Jamrozik, 2015
Figs. 35, 36 Diagrams by Julia Jamrozik and Coryn Kempster overlaid on details from drawing by Le Corbusier. Fondation Le Corbusier, Plan FLC 29364. Drawing © F.L.C. / ADAGP, Paris / Artists Rights Society (ARS), New York 2021
Figs. 37–73 Photos by Coryn Kempster and Julia Jamrozik, 2015

Lessons from Childhoods in Iconic Homes, pp. 307–317
Figs. 1–11 Photos by Coryn Kempster and Julia Jamrozik, 2015

Index

"Too many otherwise solid books about the Bible sound as if they are speaking about it from outside, from some distance. Uche Anizor's *The Goodness of God in the Gift of Scripture* speaks from inside, from a place of deep insight into how God gives Scripture to draw us near. This book is a major spiritual corrective in a modest devotional package."

Fred Sanders, Professor of Theology, Torrey Honors College, Biola University

"Uche Anizor skillfully presents the Bible as a gift to be opened and eagerly received, an extension of the God who breathed it out. Like all gifts, the Scriptures are not owed to us but freely given out of God's love and grace, inviting people to know him. This book—packaged beautifully with illustrations, quotes, and stirring hymns—invites readers to unwrap the treasures of hope, strength, wisdom, warnings, and more that are found in the Scriptures."

Colleen D. Searcy, Bible teacher; minister; author and creator, the Meet Me in the Bible series and workshops

"The apostle Paul inquires, 'What do you have that you did not receive?' (1 Cor. 4:7). We rightly reply, 'Nothing whatsoever,' then give God thanks for every good gift: creation, our very lives, the grace of salvation, our churches, and much more. Uche Anizor provocatively wonders if we would put the Bible on that list. We *receive* it. It's the word *from God.* But Anizor challenges us if we find applying and submitting to the Bible difficult because we don't truly believe that it is a good gift from God to us. If you long to embrace the Bible as a grace, a gift that stimulates your love for and thankfulness to God, then this book is for you."

Gregg R. Allison, Professor of Christian Theology, The Southern Baptist Theological Seminary; Secretary, Evangelical Theological Society

"God's word is indeed the gift that keeps on giving, straight from the mouth of our kind and generous God. *The Goodness of God in the Gift of Scripture* will stir your thinking, kindle your affections, and increase your gratitude for the Bible and all the ways that God intends to use it to nourish your soul. I highly recommend this book to you."

Kristen Wetherell, author, *Help for the Hungry Soul* and the For the Bible Tells Me So board book series

"Uche Anizor writes with a rare combination of theological depth, pastoral warmth, and practical clarity. In this book, he invites us to see the Scriptures not as a burdensome duty but as a gracious gift through which we experience the goodness of God. This is theology for discipleship: rich in truth, stirring in devotion, and practical for everyday life. I highly recommend it."

Jeremy Treat, Pastor for Preaching and Vision, Reality LA, Los Angeles, California; Professor of Theology, Biola University; author, *The Crucified King*; *Seek First*; and *The Atonement*

"Uche Anizor has again blessed the church with a book that is simple enough to pass on to a new Christian yet insightful enough to bless the seasoned Christian. By showing readers that Scripture is an expression of God's goodness that transforms our lives in so many ways, these twenty meditations are a wonderful addition to a Christian's personal time in Bible reading and prayer, a family's supper-time oral reading, or a group devoted to study and worship. Who wouldn't want such gifts as blessedness, freedom from shame, peace, nourishment, life, joy, righteousness, hope—among the many other gifts that come from immersing ourselves in God's word? Throughout my reading, I found myself captivated by insights I hadn't noticed before, drawn into worship at the wonder of our great salvation, and thankful for the way this book further stoked my passion for God's word."

Ian J. Vaillancourt, Professor of Old Testament and Hebrew, Heritage Theological Seminary; author, *Unfolding Redemption*